In Search of Competence

The Incompetent and Sometimes
Illegal Black Art of Management

JACK FEENEY (MIQA, BA-MGMT, DIP QA) is a production engineer
trained in quality and business management. After working
in the Irish print industry he moved to the USA
as an operations manager in business strategy and
development. He returned to Ireland in 1999
to project manage a multi-million dollar re-engineering
initiative with an international software company.
'One year and $1.2 million in management consulting
fees later, the company exploded spectacularly.
It was not my fault.'

In Search of Competence
The Incompetent and Sometimes Illegal Black Art of Management

Jack Feeney

The Collins Press

Published in 2004 by
The Collins Press,
West Link Park,
Doughcloyne,
Wilton,
Cork

Jack Feeney has asserted his moral right to be identified as author of this work.

British Library Cataloguing in Publication data.

Feeney, Jack
        In Search of Competence : the incompetent and sometimes
        illegal black art of management
        1. Management - Humour
        I. Title
        658'.00207

        ISBN 1903464471

Printed in Ireland by Woodprintcraft

CONTENTS

Dedicated to Maria

INTRODUCTION

Some managers are born incompetent; some acquire incompetence, while others have incompetence thrust upon them.

In a recent management survey, 71 per cent of office employees interviewed rated their manager as incompetent. This percentage figure fell to 53 per cent when skilled workers were interviewed but back to 80 per cent when semi-state employees were asked to rate their manager.

In one UK study, 'personality clashes' or 'general dissatisfaction with management' was the single biggest reason for people quitting their jobs. Management certainly has a lot to answer for but does management incompetence present a barrier or threshold to the manager of the twenty-first century? Definitely not! In fact, it's quite the contrary – many have turned incompetence into a veritable art form, an expression of their individuality and an extension of their operational 'style'.

Globally, business and management is being morally, ethically and financially scrutinised, more and more. Daily, it appears under the public microscope amid a myriad of tribunals, investigations and scandals. Management rot probably always existed and was probably always there but it has certainly been opened up to further scrutiny through phenomenal technological evolution (the internet, email, mobile phones, satellite communications, etc.)

From television, radio, newspapers and magazines, we all know what shenanigans were happening at the top of so-called, respectable organisations but what about the one's that got away? And what about the middle management in the ones that were caught – what role did THEY have in their company's demise? Did they always and genuinely believe 'people' to be their greatest asset, or were people simply a means to a grubby and seedy end? Were they comfortable to abdicate their responsibilities for people, to a department of quasi-behaviouralists, called Human Resource Management? And if they were serious about business success, why would they delegate and abdicate one of the most strategic aspects of management, namely attracting and selecting new organisational blood, to recruitment consultants, agencies and other parasitic, unprincipled life forms of the business world?

In Search of Competence is a microcosm of a bigger and greater phenomenon – management. It's about why they do, what they do, and when they do it!

Why downsize? Why expand? Why visit a management guru? Will removal of an HRM department from an organisation have any consequences? What dirty and seedy practices exist in the unsavoury world of recruitment? It's widely accepted that accountants are the most boring individuals on the face of the planet earth but how important is this in business and management? What is good service, what is good quality and what's the difference between a management guru and a circus clown?

If you've ever wondered about management, if you've ever questioned the ability of your manager, if you've ever felt uncomfortable about management or if you've ever felt your manager was talking out of the wrong orifice, this delightful, short but rich A to Z, will provide many of the answers and a fleeting insight into the incompetent and sometimes illegal, black art of management!

Chapter 1: A is for Attitude

America is the very heart of capitalism, free enterprise and good management practice (GMP). The American people love someone with that UNSTOPPABLE ATTITUDE. Get knocked down, get up, brush yourself off and try it again – if at first you don't succeed, try, try and try again.

However, in Ireland the 'valley of the squinting windows' still exists in business and management. There's bitching and envy associated with success and an almost dirty association with failure – 'I knew he was wrong from the start, but sure, there's no telling that jerk anything ...', 'He's thick ...', and so on.

But Nietzsche was right – out of chaos comes order, comes chaos and out of failure, flowers success. The great engineer and inventor Alexander Graham Bell probably had many electrical appliances literally blow up in his face before tasting sweet success with the now common telephone.

However, before receiving your management stripes you've got to understand management theory and that, at the end of the day, *it's basically bullshit*. But don't take my word for it – talk privately to virtually any publisher of management books and you will, without failure, unearth the attitude, 'Isn't it incredible how this crap sells?'

Better again, corner a management consultant, fill him or her up with alcohol and there's a high probability they'll admit the same thing. Even those who have fired hundreds of people in the name of some sub-moronic theory (downsizing, rightsizing, re-engineering) will blush awkwardly when asked how 'intellectual' management theory is. Eventually, when you get to the core issue, the word *bullshit* will always appear. Not all of it may actually be bullshit, but enough of it to qualify the rest.

In some cases management consultants can be blamed, offering organisational re-engineering transformations for € 50,000 in three days – this week only! However, consultants make convenient scapegoats – the real issue is that there are grave doubts about management theory overall. Dig deep into any area of management theory and you'll eventually arrive at bullshit. Why? Because THE WHOLE CONCEPT OF MANAGEMENT THEORY IS FUNDAMENTALLY FLAWED. If you want to understand management, you must first understand the reasons why it's flawed.

1. It is incapable of self-criticism. Because it's a nebulous and non-defined area, practically everything can be bucketed under management. Add in an element of time to bad management and everything is okay.

> *Oh yeah, it's easy to be critical of that initiative in hindsight, but at the time we were in a different commercial environment with a different set of external forces.*

In this way any management initiative can be justified – for example, you could say that the success of the Third Reich demonstrated how exceptional teamwork and cohesive synergy can work in meeting objectives of global proportion.

The *Challenger* space shuttle disaster needed to happen so that management could improve basic quality protocols. Seven astronauts were atomised on take-off on live television but if it didn't happen, who's to know what disaster could have happened?

The DeLorean failure in Belfast in 1979, which cost the British government £250 million, needed to happen so that government investors would be a little more critical the next time they handed over a large amount of cash to an executive lunatic. We just need enough time afterwards and we can rationalise any management initiative!

2. It has a greater tendency to confuse than to educate. If you manage to finish this book, you'll be as well informed about management as any management consultant. It's jargon, buzzword, cliché, acronym and fad.

3. It states the obvious in an uncommon way. Add an element of time to any management theory and you'll make a startling insight – it's all friggin' common sense. Many things that strike us nowadays as blatantly obvious were anything but that when far-sighted management theorists began to talk about them. Shakespeare once wrote that 'comedy was tragedy with the addition of time.' In a similar vein, *bullshit is management theory without the addition of time.* It's only after the event that it reaches definition.

4. It's faddish. Many management theorists haven't really looked at whether it's better to be global or local, big or small or whether business should be run in the interests of shareholders, stakeholders, customers, suppliers or society as a whole. Usually they'll advise management to do a little bit of everything under the umbrella of the latest fad, be that re-engineering, six-sigma, Just-in-Time, Total Quality Management, blah, blah, blah.

Management theory is basically the same old crap over and over again, but as a manager you must be able to talk the talk as well as walk the walk. Later in the book, buzzwords, clichés, acronyms and general management filler material will be discussed in ass-clenching detail.

With a thorough understanding of management theory and the right never-say-die attitude, it's time to go and ask someone to provide finance for your business.

However, there's no point going into your bank manager or financial lender, mouthing off big time and swinging your new-found genitalia all over the place, if you don't have a concise business plan. FAIL TO PLAN, THEN PLAN TO FAIL. You have to know not just the plot but also your lines, inside out and back to front.

You need a collection of your thoughts, a vision for the future, a plan of action. YOU NEED A BUSINESS PLAN.

CHAPTER 2: B IS FOR BUSINESS PLAN

A business plan is simply a written report on your ideas, aspirations and figures for the future of your business. Don't be afraid of it – there's no point defecating yourself at this stage of the great management journey. Ask those who would be reading your business plan (the bank manager, his or her partner, their kids) what they would like to read in any business plan before you finish and submit it. Basically, give them what they want. *You may think it's a load of nonsense, but that may be exactly what they want!* There are four basic requirements of the business plan.

1. An outline of the company's goals and aims, which should enable you to clarify your ideas. Your ideas could be insane, dangerous or just not thought through. The business plan will help you clarify your goals and objectives.

2. It should create a framework for the business' first three to five years. In turn this will enable you to draw up a structure and an operating plan. Fill in the gaps with waffle, acronyms and buzzwords *(see Chapter 3: Consultant).*

3. When it comes to getting funding from any source, it will help to impress your bank manager, potential shareholder or hotel car park venture capitalist. The projected numbers in the business plan indicate the cash flows in and out of your business for the first three to five years. Forecasting is never accurate so just pick numbers off the top of your head, double them and put them into a smart-looking chart. Everyone loves charts.

4. Finally, the business plan is a measuring stick, something you can refer back to and check and see if business is progressing. If business is not going as initially forecast, you'll spot it by constantly reviewing the plan. This will allow you enough time to strip some assets, move some cash and get the hell out of there fast if the whole thing is going belly up.

There are several fabulous books specifically written on business plans. There are also idiot-proof step-by-step booklets available from government training bodies/authorities.

Author's Tip:
Try out a few different typefaces on the business plan with a few different bank managers, politicians or organised crime leaders and watch their reaction. Don't make the plan too hairy, but make *it hairy enough to excite. If it's dull and boring, consultants can always be called in to put a bit of meat on the bone and a bit of hair on the bald spots. A good multimedia, web-enabled presentation of your business plan can have people literally lathered up into a frenzied sweat of excitement in five minutes.*

B is also for bullshit, the very cornerstone of management. Some people are naturals but anyone can learn, as the whole management concept is ill defined and open to abuse. Start your apprenticeship by sending memorandums ('memos' for short) to friends and family.

It's obviously very important that memos contain lots of important buzzwords. What the memos actually say isn't particularly important. In the real world, if it was important someone would discuss it in person. The procedure is simple. Think of any three-digit number and then select the corresponding buzzword from each column below.

For instance, number 257 produces 'systematised logistical projection', a phrase that can be dropped into virtually any memo, report or conversation with a sincere ring of decisive, knowledgeable authority. No one will have the remotest idea of what you're talking about, but the important thing is that they are not about to admit it.

Column 1	Column 2	Column 3
0. integrated	0. management	0. options
1. heuristic	1. organisational	1. flexibility
2. systematised	2. monitored	2. capability
3. parallel	3. reciprocal	3. mobility
4. functional	4. digital	4. programming
5. responsive	5. logistical	5. scenarios
6. optional	6. transitional	6. time-phase
7. synchronised	7. incremental	7. projection
8. compatible	8. third-generation	8. hardware
9. futuristic	9. policy	9. contingence

After a couple of weeks of practice and having read this book, you'll notice yourself bullshitting more and more and *talking crap with confidence.*

Chapter 3: C is for Consultant

There are consultants for literally everything and if business is growing and you've got plenty of funds, you'll attract them like dung beetles to faeces. Be careful meeting them initially, as you may be later invoiced for the meeting or conversation. Try hanging a carrot in front of them, no strings attached, just meeting them for a chat and then book an expensive restaurant.

Consultants will never miss an opportunity for a free lunch. Lace them with alcohol and then run your ideas by them. For the price of a good (tax-deductible) lunch, you'll receive your first consultation free of charge!

Even if you haven't a clue what you or your business is about, you could always use a few generic clichés to make an 'informed' comment on any management situation. Avoid specifics and detail and always avoid writing anything down.

'Well, what goes up must come down', 'What goes around comes around', 'No point counting chickens till they're hatched', etc., etc. Learn as many business clichés as your head will allow and practice using them, initially on family and friends and then on staff below you in the organisation. If you get the whole language totally screwed up, it's only your minions that see your incompetence. Total denial of the whole conversation later on is also possible with subordinates.

C IS ALSO FOR CONSOLIDATION and this is the opposite to fragmentation. If you're fragmented, consolidate and if you're consolidated, fragment. The whole concept is not as important as bringing it up at the right moment in conversation. For example: 'We're up shit creek and we need to consolidate our resources, people and key competencies' one day, and, 'We've got to break up this baby fast or she's gonna pull us all down' on another day. Both work equally well in management.

Consultants can add a fresh stimulus to any organisation but you've got to keep an eye on them. If you don't, you may be still working on the same project five years later with nothing to show but a few grant payments. If you do feel the need to hire consultants (to reduce your tax burden, for instance) make sure:

- They're covered by some handout government grant.
- They have an established base of customers and an established field of speciality.
- The terms of engagement and project scope are defined, agreed and signed off by both parties – before they start living it up on your credit cards.
- They have no connections to organised crime, human resource management or recruitment consultants.

C IS ALSO FOR CLOTHING. Clothing is important and one should always dress to impress. For men, the charcoal suit is nearly always appropriate. Women can now dress in similar 'say nothing' clothing but can colour the situation with a little make-up. Not too much, though – whatever the business situation, no manager ever wants to look like a pasty air hostess. It's generally not a good idea for men to wear make-up in business unless the business requires them to do so.

USE CASH FOR ALL TRANSACTIONS – there's no trail or evidence later on if you have to attend a tribunal or investigation. This is now a common enough aspect of Irish management and business.

CHAPTER 4: D IS FOR DELEGATION AND DOWNSIZE

Delegation is more than just giving some task you can't be bothered your ass dealing with to a subordinate – it's an integral part of management.

As a manager you won't want to send a racehorse down a coal pit to do the job of a pit pony, nor will you want to race a pit pony. Good managers know what tasks to delegate and what tasks not to delegate.

By continually delegating, you're sending out a powerful management message to all those in the organisation – you're in control, trust them and YOU ARE A MANAGER.

AUTHOR'S TIP:

Whether you're managing racehorses, pit ponies or human resources (people), always keep a firm grip on the reigns but don't sit on them when they're carrying out their task. So what if they screw *things up big time – nothing that can't be fixed. However, if they're continually screwing up, there are two options, depending on the incumbent's contract status:*

1. FIRE THEM. If they're still on a six-month probationary period (see Chapter 5: Expansion), firing them couldn't be easier. Simply grab their attention and then point to the door or closest exit. Tell them you'll mail their tax forms. This gives you

> *enough time, two weeks or so, for possible repercussions.*
>
> *2. DOWNSIZE. This is even more fun than firing! When you're too heavy as a human resource/person, you need to bring your weight down to acceptable limits through a change in diet and/or a more frequent exercise plan.*

Business, too, gets bloated, fat and ugly and when this translates into a financial loss, you may need to downsize, perform a turn-around and lose some fat. Management consultants prefer the term 'rightsize', which hints at some almost normal and natural evolutionary phase of business, but it's the same thing. If your business is slow, stupid and missing market opportunities, you downsize it.

The first step in downsizing is removing at least one senior manager – just to send out the right message. If there's a potential cash flow crisis, make cash your number one priority – cash is and always will be king.

1. Meet the bank manager and let them know of your plans to downsize. Lather them well with comprehensive head count plans and projected cash flow charts. EVERYONE LOVES CHARTS.

2. Meet individually with creditors/suppliers, update them of your plan and advise them that heads will roll but they will in no way lose out. Always understate the extent of your problems with creditors/suppliers – the last thing you want is for them to call in all outstanding credit.

3. Focus efforts on collecting existing customer debts and overall try to take in as much cash as possible while simultaneously paying out as little as possible. Additionally, adopt a selective policy with creditors in relation to who you actually pay. *If they're big and rich, they can probably wait.*

4. Terminate the employment of all temporary staff immediately. If you've got a human resource department, get rid of it. In fact, eliminate all departments, functions and roles that don't add value to the product or service you're selling.

5. Suspend non-essential expenses until further notice. If you're having your office refurnished, a pool put in your garden or a boat put on your car, hold back, at least until the dust settles.

6. Make all recruitment subject to your approval. It should be that way anyway, but do it just in case.

7. Eliminate any lavish entertainment or visible extravagance. This sends out the right message – even the *head honcho*, the *main man*, the *big cheese, el numero uno* is prepared to cut back. It follows that everyone else in the organisation will do likewise.

8. Establish at least three profitability projects within the organisation and staff the projects with cross-functional teams. Allow them the autonomy to expedite actions, initiate improvements and report back to you on progress. Crises are always a major turning point in any organisation's fortune; and can be great fun.

The evidence shows that surgery and short-term profit-improvement actions are likely to eliminate losses, but that major new initiatives are needed to achieve an acceptable financial return. Although we use the word surgery, this is far from brain surgery. In fact, all of the above measures are nothing more than common sense and can be carried out even if the company is not up the creek.

For the organisational surgeon, the trick is to remove as little muscle but as much fat as possible – *it's organisational liposuction* without removing or damaging any vital organs.

AUTHOR'S TIP:
Instead of going on a roller -coaster corporate crash diet, keep your organisation crisis free and financially healthy by downsizing at least twice a year! Don't wait till the horse has bolted – it's *your horse and your business. Many managers wait until the horse has gone completely out of control before taking remedial and corrective action. Don't wait – downsize regularly and keep the organisation fit and healthy.*

Downsizing presents a great opportunity to fix every rotting ailment in the organisation and clear out all those deadheads you took on last year when business was booming and expanding like a mad thing.

However, before downsizing or rightsizing, you'll first need to expand.

CHAPTER 5: E IS FOR EXPANSION

When things take off and confidence is high you may wish to expand your business through an injection of cash. In Ireland there's the Business Expansion Scheme (BES) that's been around since 1984. It's aimed mostly at expanding companies, but open to abuse and a major source of legitimate tax evasion in the hands of the 'right accountant'.

BES funding is an attractive alternative to dealing with a venture capitalist. You won't wake up with your knees in a plastic bag if you miss a payment and your family will never be dragged from their beds in the middle of the night.

There is no minimum turnover or profitability stipulation but the company selected for funding must have the ability to pay back to the agreed terms. A good business plan with three to five year sales, cash and cost projections will demonstrate this ability even if it's a complete work of fiction.

The BES is well worth looking into. Even if you're not an expanding company, you can say you are and take your chances. Use a 'well-greased' accountant.

There's nothing to lose and everything to gain. Once you've got the funds, you can then expand your human resources. These are basically people, but calling them human resources, or HR, makes the whole thing a lot less personal when you're downsizing on a regular basis.

A recent survey of Irish chief executive officers (real big shots) revealed that two of the most significant problems in trying to implement a business strategy were not having the right people capable of delivering the strategy and a failure to train people effectively. The survey concluded that buildings, equipment and machinery, light and heat, etc., had LESS of an impact on strategy than people!

With expansion funds in your pocket and mind-blowing management research in your head, start hiring those human resources essential for expansion.

However, a word of advice – play your cards very close to your chest. If it's widely known that you're on the lookout for staff, you may find recruitment consultants hanging around your basement car park or turning up in your local supermarket, CVs in hand. They can be extremely difficult to shake off.

AUTHOR'S TIP:
Buy a Doberman.

INTERVIEWING HUMAN RESOURCES

Interviewing is easy and involves just a few basic skills. There are many good books published on style and technique and step-by-step manuals for accountants, recruitment consultants and people working in human resource management departments. With the proper checklists, procedures and job description, a well-trained chimp could carry out the interview. However, it's always better that you yourself carry out the interview.

Good planning and preparation is always essential, for both the interviewee and the interviewer. Always meet the employee face to face.

If you don't want the interview to last more than twenty minutes, set your mobile phone alarm to go off appropriately and just pretend you're being called away to something urgent.

If you want to test the candidate's general wherewithal, don't have the phone ring. Just stand up, stare at them, maintain fixed eye contact and walk out of the office. Return ten minutes later and ask them to provide an explanation as to what *they feel* actually happened. Take notes on their response. Always take notes, or at least maintain the appearance of taking notes, throughout the interview. *You may only be doodling on a blank sheet but make out like it's really important.*

Panel interviews are great fun if you can muster up eight or ten 'business' people, and better again if you combine candidate participative role play. Have the interviewee sit in the middle of the room and the panel gathered in a semi-circle around their chair.

Better again, with twelve interviewers, have the panel completely circle the interviewee at intervals of 30 degrees. This may make the interviewee slightly uncomfortable, but making them comfortable isn't what this is about. Remember, it's your money you're going to invest in taking them on.

Written psychometric and think-blot testing are the very cornerstone of all interviews. Use them. They throw a bit of structure and formality on the whole thing but also alert you as to the interviewee being a nutter, dangerous or a private investigator connected to a recruitment firm.

When it comes to discussing salary and remuneration, just say, 'It's an attractive package and all our money is clean'. That'll always stop the salary/wages conversation dead in its tracks.

Finally, never give anyone a signed and written contract of employment. If you're being dragged by the ass through the labour courts later on, less is always more.

With written contracts, procrastination is always a good way to avoid making a commitment. Just keep putting them off indefinitely.

Regarding the law, all new employees should carry out a six-month probationary period with the employer before they become organisational furniture. Once the six months are up, there's a legal obligation on the employer to review the person and either make the employee permanent or frogmarch them off the premises.

The human resource has limited rights when on probation, so try and keep them there for as long as possible. There are plenty of options open to the manager to keep people on probation – indefinitely!

1. Review them, find their performance 'below par' (they won't know what the hell you're talking about), and then extend their probationary period for a further three months. This way you keep them in limbo, pending your satisfaction. They'll still have minimal rights, the same as if they were on probation!

2. Review them one week before their six-month probationary period is over, tell them business is bad, present a fictional set of business figures and a made-up business plan, and then tell them you've got to let them go but may take them back on when business picks up. You then simply re-hire them the following week and start a whole new six-month probationary phase.

AUTHOR'S TIP:

*If you've hired someone for your organisation,
regardless of what they do, tell the world your
business exists through the 'People on the Move'
announcements in business sections of national newspapers.*

It's cheap advertising and if you can convince the new employee to wear a sombrero or a false beard and glasses, it'll be sure to raise the general awareness of your business.

Only in Ireland do the national daily newspapers advertise movements in middle management. Outside of Ireland, people at the peak of their very successful professional careers appear in specialised trade publications. Their career movements affect industry, commerce and society. Check out the Irish 'people on the move' sections – you're guaranteed a laugh, and if you're looking for a cheap publicity stunt, there's none better. For example:

PEOPLE ON THE MOVE!
Steve Morley has just been appointed Customer Delight manager

with Pilfrey, Pilfrey and Monkey, a Firm of exciting management accountants. Customers are currently delighted with the firm, but Steve will sustain and develop that delight even further. He holds a couple of certificates in management and stuff, is a lead assessor for ISO9000, has a collection of over 50 pocket calculators and talks management like there's no tomorrow.

Married to Chardonnay, the couple have

two cats, Gordon and Gecko, a calf, three sheep, sixteen hens and live in a Winabago camper van on the outskirts of Dublin. Relocation will not present a problem. Steve's waist size is 32" while his inside leg measurement is 34". For relaxation he enjoys origami, talking on his mobile and working on his novel - *A Man on the Move.*

Steve's new employer, Pilfrey, Pilfrey and Monkey, is wet with excitement at having poached Steve from a competing firm of accountants, Walfrey, Walfrey and Mongey, and wish him every success in his new position!

As you grow and expand your business, don't forget to keep an eye on finances.

CHAPTER 6: F IS FOR FINANCE

While it's always important to be prudent in business, it's important not to get bogged down with financial detail. Learn about a few key performance indicators (KPIs to management consultants) and steer the business from afar. Three good ones are:

1. Cost. If you're taking in more revenue than is going out in cost, it's a good thing – this is the cost:revenue ratio. No rocket science here.

2. Inventory/stock. How often does the stock/materials you purchased turn in a normal business year? If you've got a warehouse the size of an aircraft hangar, you're in trouble. In buying groceries for the home, it's generally not a good idea to buy a year's supply in one fell swoop. The very same rationale applies in business – buy frequently, buy small volumes and never buy on the basis of price alone, even if the supplier has given you a few good nights at a lap-dancing joint, or a cash 'political donation' wrapped in an old newspaper.

3. Service. If a customer makes an order for goods or services and doesn't see hide nor tail of you for a year, they won't be happy. Measure how happy customers are – use a private investigator or a management consultant to gauge the happiness of your customer. The best indication of customer satisfaction is business growth, though Irish banking is a general exception to this rule.

If the service you're providing is good and continually improving, it's likely that more and more people will want to do business with you. It's the ultimate acid test. Service management is extensive – so much so that an entire chapter of this book is dedicated to it. (See Chapter 19: S is for service management)

Once you keep an eye on the key performance indicators (KPIs), you can leave the books to the accountants. If your business can afford a full-time accountant, great! With the right accountant, you can basically put everything financial through the books – mortgage, car expenses, holidays, theatre, cinema, training, clothing, electricity, kids' education, Christmas presents, food and drink, lap dancing, gambling, paintballing – there's literally no limit once you hold onto receipts!

If you can't afford a full-time accountant, you can always have one of them fix the books before handing in your tax return. However, it's a lot easier if you can drip feed them receipts throughout the year.

Accountants serve a long, highly ritualistic and mind-numbing apprenticeship, but it's possible to pick them up fresh and without baggage, for minimum wage, when they're struggling with exams, rituals, paintball weekends, etc.

AUTHOR'S TIP:
Look for accountants about to qualify and
when interviewing them, emphasise 'supporting
their career training' as opposed to remunera-
tion (money). When they've signed on the dotted line and
you've got them on minimum wage, the 'career support'
could turn out to be no more than the provision of a desk,

> *calculator-watch and a library card. The majority of trainee accountants will jump at the chance of an employer offering 'career support'.*

Once snared, you simply train them up as you want them, monitoring, feeding and watering them appropriately. They won't need a whole lot of supervision, but for the first year or so they will be constantly having you approve the most trivial detail.

Accountants are highly motivated by trivia and detail. As a performance-related bonus, give them a (tax-deductible) turkey and ham for Christmas – that'll keep them happy for another year.

An accountant with his Christmas bonus.

Accountants can be trained to do almost anything as long as there's no creativity or innovation required. Train them to keep a minimum of two sets of accounts, which although different, all add up to the same final balances. If you need to siphon off some cash for a new car, plane or Spanish villa, use accounts number two. Accounts number one will be what you give to the taxman. A third set of accounts could be prepared for the boardroom coffee table or the table in your business reception area. This third set will be extremely hairy and show the world how charitably you spend your profits. They'll show how you and your company help downtrodden coffee growers in South America unite, how you promote the use of non-fossil fuels and how you educate the masses.

Once you've trained your accountant and they've settled into their mind-numbing routine, they'll last for years and years. Routine is of paramount importance to accountants. They'll use the toilet on the hour, every hour, without fail. They'll literally cover their office space with yellow post-its reminding them of things to do and when they have to be done by. Their desks are always clean and will always have a black pen, a red pen, a ruler, a calculator and, for the more adventurous, an executive toy (Newton's Cradle or equivalent).

Socially, accountants don't mix very well with other members of the human race and many would say it's easier to hold a conversation with a rabbit than it is with an accountant. However, if the conversation is about accounts, tax or payroll, they'll talk and talk and talk to the point of catatonic stupor.

Accountants discussing accounts, tax and payroll.

It's widely known that many accountants keep ant farms and will spend hour upon hour tending to their flock and even talking with the little creatures. Yet it's this obsessive, compulsive and anal disorder that ensures that if anyone's dipping their bread in your gravy, you'll be the first to know it.

Up until the Celtic Tiger blossomed (note: use of mixed metaphors is perfectly acceptable language as a manager), most accountants were reasonably straight, being governed by a strict code of professional practice and Mooney-like initiation ceremonies.

Post-Celtic Tiger, things have changed and even accountants are being investigated through tribunals. A tribunal is similar to a US Senate hearing or war crimes tribunal where a court and judge examine and review information and evidence put before it and make a judgement. The final judgement could be a recommendation to change operating protocols/procedures, the imposition of a fine or in extreme cases, a jail sentence and/or public flogging. That's the theory, but in Ireland no one is ever disciplined. Never underestimate the power of waffle, selective amnesia and all cash transactions being 'political donations', regardless of how 'dirty' or 'seedy' they appear.

The Blaney tribunal (named after Judge Blaney) was set up in 1997 to investigate the 'professional and business competence of some of the country's leading accountants'. There are many accountants worried and for obvious reasons, many clenched asses pending the outcome of the tribunal. However, they should relax those sphincters – no doubt Blarney will beat Blaney!

CHAPTER 7: G IS FOR GURU

<u>Are you</u> willing to confront the unique leadership challenges caused by the expanding complexity and chaos of changing organisational life?

<u>Are you</u> searching to gain a rare insight into the complexity of strategic leadership and find proactive strategies for rapid, radical changes in business?

<u>And are you</u> serious about building leadership capabilities, fostering innovation and supporting positive change to meet the challenge of today's high-pressure environment?

If you answered 'yes' to at least one of the above questions, you may have GURU-DEFICIT SYNDROME (GDS) and may need to seek help.

Management gurus are the main movers, the big shakers, the *honcho monchos*, the group of individuals specialised and experienced in the highest levels of organisation and management evolution. *Fortune* magazine talks of the ur-guru while *The Economist* talks about the uber-guru. These are people at the very peak of guru-dom.

The management guru is the one whom all managers look to for inspiration, creativity and a quick fix. It's widely known that most people working in human resource management even pray to some management gurus.

Academic gurus will describe an organisational scenario/ situation in mind-numbing detail and if nothing else will cause the manager to do something he or she would not have done otherwise – to think. However, expect no quick fix with the academic guru. One must wade through volumes of waffle and common sense before encountering clarity and any 'eureka' moment.

Management gurus (or MUGS, as they're called) are a totally different kettle of fish. Mugs always use words like challenging, chaotic, insightful, proactive, radical, fostering, innovative, etc., etc. If you were playing *bullshit bingo* (see Chapter 13: Management) with them, you'd have a jackpot every five minutes.

Waffle and bullshit aside, is organisational life really more chaotic, complex and challenging than it was at the very dawn of civilisation? Five thousand years ago, the Egyptian pharaohs built the pyramids, co-ordinating over 50,000 slaves (human resources) in a project spanning over 100 years. They applied feats of engineering impossible to reproduce even in today's world. They built structures that have challenged the ravages of time. Nowadays, we're still unravelling mathematical and astronomical insights into the pyramids and their alignment with the planets. Was their project simple, non-challenging and carried out in an ordered fashion? I don't think so. Nor do I think the pharaohs had large HRM departments.

Closer to the present, Mr Henry Ford revolutionised management application through his linear mass production model in the early twentieth century. Through hard work, analysis and practical thinking, Ford streamlined his operations to such a degree that his factory produced a fully functioning Model T Ford in 104 hours.

This included processing his own iron ore, moulding pre-assemblies, joining assemblies, pulling the whole thing together and driving it off the line. All in less than a week, with only a handful of people dying or being mutilated/disfigured by the process! Was this not complex, challenging and chaotic? Modern-day managers will add that the Model T was only available in black, but then again, is that not what the market wanted? Management could learn a lot from Mr Ford!

The management challenges faced nowadays are no more complex or chaotic than the challenges we faced since we first stood upright as a species. Sure, we now demand more, but satisfying increasing demand has been made a lot easier through quantum and incremental leaps in technology and communications (electricity, telephone, radio, satellite, super microprocessors, PDAs, laptops, home PCs, etc., etc.).

Management is no more complex nor life more chaotic than it was in the past, but gurus will insist we are living in exceptional times. But every time in the present or future is exceptional, simply because we haven't been there yet!

One of the greatest management thinkers and writers of the twentieth century, Henry Mintzberg, once wrote, 'Why does every generation have to think that it lives in the period with the greatest turbulence?' Benjamin Disraeli, noted statesman and novelist, once stated, 'It is the fashion to style the present moment an extraordinary crisis!' THE PRESENT IS INDEED EXTRAORDINARY.

Management gurus are powerful, larger-than-life figures in our society and despite talking a lot of rhetoric and cliché, they do affect the way we see ourselves and our business. An effective manager knows the main gurus and their philosophies inside out and is never caught off guard at a cocktail party with an unfamiliar model.

Author's Tip:

Read this book twice and become a management *guru! You'll make loads of money and anyone working in human resource management will literally kiss your ass. For people working in HRM, management gurus are preaching bishops while paint balling is the equivalent of going to mass.*

Chapter 8: H is for Human Resource Management

As you grow and build your business, office, expense account and lifestyle, you may notice a strange phenomenon developing – a human resource management department sprouts out of literally nowhere.

The single greatest conceptual flaw of twenty-first century management is human resource management, the belief that people are a separate side of management, and that strategy is in a different silo. We've all heard managers chant the mantra *'people are our greatest asset'– people are the organisation's only asset!* A great leader, Abraham Lincoln, once wrote, 'Labour is prior to, and independent of, capital. Capital is only the fruit of labour, and could never have existed if labour had not first existed. Labour is superior to capital, and deserves much the higher consideration.'

Human resource management (HRM) evolved from personnel management, which evolved from a worker representation role.

The initial role had some basis and credibility, offering literate representation to the illiterate non-managerial worker. Worker reps were also responsible for crow-barring brawling employees on behalf of management. They bridged the gap between management and non-management. This provided a worthwhile contribution to the organisation, ending quarrels and disputes in the most timely and cost-effective manner.

Seeing the benefits of abdicating part of their responsibility, management developed the worker representative role further, called it personnel management and moved more and more people issues in the direction of the personnel department. Slowly but surely, more and more people issues were abdicated to the personnel department who now resolved stalemates, settled grievances, formalised agreements between management and non-management and fed back reports to management on the motivational status of their employees. This allowed general management to concentrate and commit their focus to the real management issues of improving output, production, turnover, profitability, etc. In doing so, they abdicated the most important aspect of management – people.

Over time, the management of people became less of a general management issue and more of a personnel issue. Through more time and subtle, incremental change, personnel management became a competing management role within the organisational domain. Personnel managers were then elevated to the same level as the production manager, the finance manager, the sales manager, etc., perceived as an integral part of the overall management. Now on equal footing with other functional roles, it deserved a new title and the term 'human resource management' was born.

THE RISE IN HRM IS DIRECTLY PROPORTIONAL TO THE DECLINE IN GENERAL MANAGEMENT'S UNDERSTANDING OF MANAGEMENT! General management has truly lost sight of its reason for existence – *to manage people.* Some established management specialists say this is part of the reason why UK productivity is 40 per cent lower than in the US.

The British Trade and Industry secretary has even appointed Michael Porter, one of the greatest academic management gurus of this and the last century, to investigate the whole phenomenon of performance management. Will HRM survive powerful intellectual and rational analysis? I don't think so!

PEOPLE ARE OUR GREATEST ASSET

People are not the organisation's greatest asset – t*hey are the* organisation's *only asset*. However, the presence and growth of the HRM movement does nothing to qualify this gem of common sense. In fact, its presence indicates quite the contrary – that management has lost sight of the very reason it exists, to manage the only true variable – people.

The HRM phenomenon is a classic example of management evolution and extrapolation between two unconnected concepts: people are our greatest asset, therefore HRM is our organisation's most strategic and critical management role. It's this simple but subtle misunderstanding that makes HRM the tower of babble that it is.

CHICKEN OR EGG CONUNDRUM – WHICH CAME FIRST?

Did successful organisations come about as a result of large HRM departments, or did large HRM departments come about as a result of the organisation's success? Judging by the companies that have large HRM departments, I would suggest the latter scenario being closer to reality.

Look around at some of the industries that have large HRM budgets and departments. Take pharmaceutical and information technology, two fat industries, profit-wise. Within these industries, HRM specialists justify their existence by their huge (so big, it's immeasurable) contribution to profitability because 'people are the organisation's greatest asset' and because 'they manage people'. Couldn't be simpler. However, what they fail to see is that it's only because the organisation is so fat (profit-wise) that it can afford to have a complete department of quasi-behaviourists dedicated toward doing Jack shit. If the organisation were not fat, it couldn't possibly afford to have an entire legion of people carrying out employee climate surveys, numerically measuring organisational unity or using external management gurus to apply questionable motivation techniques.

Look at organisations that have large HRM departments and you'll spot organisational obesity. Obese, fat companies or companies that are making super-normal profits (profits above and beyond what is required for normal business success) always find their excess fat being eaten up by activities that contribute in no way to the product or service offering.

Even in 2003 some obese, large Irish organisations had a crew of Y2K engineers on payroll just in case that 'bug thing' comes back.

FIGURE H1: ORGANISATIONAL OBESITY VS. HRM CURVE

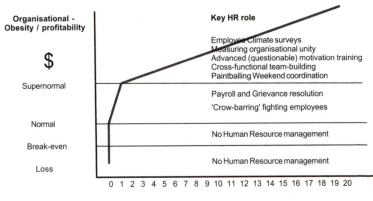

If you were to look at a more traditional but less rich industry, such as the Irish printing industry, there's a distinct absence of HRM. It will only exist as a minor function within those companies that are part of a larger group. Larger groups can afford obesity. Figure H1 demonstrates the relationship between organisational obesity and the size of the HRM department. Always keep an eye on the organisational 'waste-line'.

Overall, the more obese and profitable your organisation is, the bigger its HRM department will be.

An HRM presence simply indicates that management in some other area of the organisation has lost sight of what it's doing and probably has its vision blurred by the fact that its head is firmly locked up its own ass.

PERCEPTION IS EVERYTHING

If you place a frog into a saucepan of cold water and slowly heat the water, what happens? The frog, interpreting the warming water (environment) to be good, will doze off into a sleep, then into a coma and then die. He perceives the environment to be friendly because it's warm and comfortable, when in fact it's about to kill him. In the same way, managers will perceive their surrounding environment to be friendly when in fact it's potentially fatal. In response to a changing environment, managers will generally amplify their past actions. This only speeds up the boiling process – 'This worked well in the past so I'm sure it'll work again' – wrong! On a larger scale this phenomenon is known as the 'Icarus Paradox' and 1980s IBM or Big Blue was one of the greatest examples.

Interpret the environment correctly and look for the early signs that the organisation needs COLONIC IRRIGATION. If the organisation is getting fat, sloppy, stupid and unresponsive to customer demands or if the HR department agenda suddenly appears important, sound the alarm bells – it's time to shed some excess fat.

The initial role of HRM did fill some organisational void – crow-barring brawling employees and bridging the gap between management and non-management – but general management created the current monster by diverting people issues to the perceived organisation specialists. However, on reflection there are few management issues that don't involve people. Even the very word 'management' suggests people – what other type of management exists?

The only positive point of having a large HRM department comes about when downsizing. They make good downsize fodder and will not be missed in the normal course of business. They add no value to the good, or service provided and zero value to your customers' perception of your business!

Organisations have survived for thousands of years without HRM and will probably continue to survive for thousands more once management reclaims what it abdicated in error – people management. THE RISE IN POPULARITY OF THE HRM FUNCTION IS DIRECTLY PROPORTIONAL TO THE DECLINE IN MANAGEMENT'S FUNDAMENTAL UNDERSTANDING OF MANAGEMENT. People are not just your greatest asset, they're your only asset!

AUTHOR'S TIP:
Always downsize (rightsize!) when you see the first signs of a human resource management department developing. Hit early, hit fast and hit hard.

> *Human resource management adds no value to your product or service offering. The HRM concept gained recognition through general management lacking basic and fundamental people skills. All leaders and managers should be trained not in human resource management (cringe!), but rather in respecting people for what they actually are – people. However, common sense is not always that common, especially in the world of management.*

Human resource management is probably the greatest conceptual flaw of modern management. To call HRM a red herring in the vast sea of management is the understatement of the century, not to mention an injustice to fish. *Human resource management is nothing but the bastard love child of decaying management practice* and the Brady Bunch, on a touchy, feely paintball weekend.

Chapter 9: I is for Ignorance Management

As a leader of people, a manager must continually adapt his or her management style to a constantly changing environment. The style of leadership or management that worked brilliantly last year or even last week may not be appropriate today. A style of management highly effective today may be totally ineffective tomorrow. Indeed, management theorists will agree that no single style resists the ravages of time and no single style fits all situations. In analysing management styles, theorists put forward the following four-box style model – it's supposed to cover most possibilities.

Figure 11: Management Styles

Participative	Collaborative
Co-operative	Directive

The idea is that depending on the management situation, a participative, collaborative, co-operative or directive style of management, or a combination of styles, will resolve the situation.

In analysis of management and leadership styles, a theory called *traits theory* was developed in the 1950s. The basis of this was that all leaders demonstrated certain common characteristics. It was interesting to read but did little or nothing to define leadership.

The traits theory has since been demoted to the shelves of lunacy. If leadership were defined by simply viewing characteristics or traits, Idi Amin, Adolf Hitler, Rasputin and every other madman that walked the face of the planet would go down in history as the planet's greatest leaders. This makes sense in a screwed-up sort of way, I'm sure you'll agree.

However, let's forget about traits theory and concentrate on the impressive four-box style model above. No single style is practiced in isolation of the other styles and no single style or combination fits all situations!

Like so many other management philosophies, it's all friggin' common sense once you wade through the waffle. But what happens when all the combinations and permutations of the style model have been exhausted and a situation still exists without resolution?

Many managers will simply use an ignorance management style as a last-ditch attempt. Though very effective and frequently applied, few books and articles have captured the essence of ignorance management (IM), even though it's practiced in many organisations. The main advantage of IM over the other styles of management is its applicability in practically every situation where all other styles fail.

Below are a number of management situations or scenarios, the symptoms and the IM response and resolution.

FIGURE 12: IGNORANCE MANAGEMENT APPLICATION

Issue/Situation	Symptoms	IM Resolution
Role confusion	What am I supposed to be doing?	Whatever I say.

Issue/Situation	Symptoms	IM Resolution
Cynicism	There was nothing wrong with the old way	Then you won't mind 'old way' pay!
Holding onto the past	It was better in the old days!	As above.
Commitment from senior management	I'll change when they change!	You'll change when I say
Skills/knowledge	I'm not sure I can do this.	Do it!
Apprehension	Where am I going to get the time to do this?	That's your problem – get your act together fast or you'll have a lot more free time
Reversal to the past	Oh, that – I stopped doing that months ago – couldn't bother my ass doing that!	You'll do it now or you'll have no ass to bother!
Responsibility	It's got nothing to do with me.	It's your job – do it or I'll be downsizing fast!

The responses are only suggestions so as to grasp the fundamental concept. They should be shouted at people while the manager looks fierce and holds an important-looking folder.

Author's Tip:

Ignorance management is a powerful management tool, but the well-evolved manager should only engage the style as a last-ditch attempt at resolution. If not used in moderation, subordinates will just perceive you as an ignorant jerk, and more importantly, they'll know your style and develop counter-styles. Continually change your style of management and keep them confused. Exhibit no consistency and any counter-style measures will be diffused before the situation is allowed to escalate. The successful application of igno-

rance management is subtle, but if misapplied, can indeed back-fire. In dealing with people, the form of words and face-to-face skills of ignorance management demand thought and patience.

Some of the more common sins and cures of IM are detailed below:

FIGURE 13

SINS	CURES
What the hell have you been doing?	The manager should know everything his staff have been doing.
You're a lazy, rotting son of a bitch!	So what – it doesn't interfere with the job at hand.
Of course you've landed this on me	Be prepared for anything and everything
Those things are good so we'll leave them, but how so you explain this shit?	Analyse both success and failure.
Well, that's it for another year – now get the hell out of here!	Reviews should be ongoing and never-ending.
Well yes, that's right, but what you don't know is ...	Don't publicly trump aces.
I haven't got time to listen to this drivel.	Management should always have time to listen to their employees.

Chapter 10: J is for Job Description

A job description is just that – a description of a job, what tasks are involved, who reports into the position and who the position reports into. It should include what level of education and how many years of experience are required and most jobs will have a title, such as marketing manager, group finance director, pimp, bounty hunter, receptionist, etc. It's all basic stuff, but in a management context the job description becomes many things.

For senior management it becomes a platform to jerk off about how good it is to work for them and their company. For recruitment companies it becomes a method of gathering CVs through advertising broad and general jobs that only exist in cyber-reality.

They use job descriptions to pull in CVs for jobs that don't exist to build up their databases. Finally, for the unsuspecting job seeker, they provide one of two emotions: complete awe and fascination or total confusion.

For instance, take the following position advertised on the internet. It's for a junior recruitment executive holding a third-level business qualification with one to two years of direct selling experience. The salary for the position is 24K per annum with performance-related bonus. (Author's translations in italics.)

Location: Dublin
Start date: As soon as possible
Salary: Negotiable
Additional benefits: Training, performance-related bonus
Role(s) that best describe this job: Recruitment consultant, tele-sales executive
Job type: Permanent full time
Minimum experience required: One to two years
Minimum level of education: Third level, telephone skills
Special skills: Closing sales

JOB DESCRIPTION

Recruit Nation is one of Ireland's leading niche recruitment companies.

AUTHOR'S TRANSLATION: *Niche is always a good adjective if the company is otherwise unheard of. The niche could be the provision of recruitment services by rotting scumbags, but that in itself is still technically a niche – niche is broad, general, nebulous and nearly always appropriate.*

Due to massive success, we are expanding our sales team now and immediately require a very keen and active young sales champion to join our team.

AUTHOR'S TRANSLATION: *Massive success equals sales team expansions? Don't think so. Keen, active and young means tiny salary.*

We are a sales-focused company and strive to hunt for new business on a continual basis.

Author's translation: *Most people we deal with don't return for business a second time.*

We currently have an opening for a recruiter to join our team of sales consultants. To be considered for this fast-paced role, you must have two years' proven sales or telesales experience in direct outbound sales where you achieve by conquering new business.

Author's translation: *You'll sell stuff to people that they initially don't want. You'll leave your scruples at home! We'll always have an opening!*

You must have the ability to cold call for new accounts and you are excellent at making large numbers of outbound sales calls each day. As a person you are motivated, persistent, dedicated, hard working, with high energy levels and an outgoing personality. You'll have a professional approach to your clients and you'll have a clean-cut professional image.

Author's translation: *You'll pester people to the point of deal closure and will not be offended by a simple 'sod off and don't annoy me' phone comment or solicitor's letter. As long as you don't have one eye in the middle or your forehead, enjoy wearing a suit and tie and are clean, your image will be acceptable.*

It is expected that you have a third-level qualification, good written and verbal communication skills and basic PC skills (MS Word, e-mail, etc.).

Author's translation: *If you're interested and can write a job description like the rubbish you're reading right now, you've got the job. It's a bonus if you've got a third-level degree because we're paying peanuts.*

You will be keen to influence your own financial destiny by earning high sales commission. This is an excellent time to join an expanding company with an excellent high-energy working environment.

AUTHOR'S TRANSLATION: *Anything goes, including you.*

We pay basic salary (*minimum wage*), the best commission rates in recruitment in Ireland, provide excellent sales support and we have the best training programme in Ireland.

AUTHOR'S TRANSLATION: *All training is on the job – what better?*

Our challenge is a difficult one (*recruiters are generally challenged individuals*) and only winners should consider applying. If you desire the ultimate sales career, apply now.

DISCLAIMER: this is totally a sales-orientated role and you must have sales experience to apply. If you are seeking a role in HR or personnel this position will not be suitable for you.

APPLICATION: the recruiter is interested in your answers to the following question(s). Please place your answers in the e-mail you send when applying for the job.

1. Do you have two years' proven sales/telesales experience?
2. Are you seeking a new sales challenge – *can you put together a job description like this with less than ten spolling/grammoticalical errors?*

3. Do you get a hard-on at the very thought of closing a sale, regardless of what you're selling?

4. Have you got a clean criminal record?

5. Are you willing to invest € 500 (cash)?

If you're a job seeker, be aware that the job description may bear no resemblance to the actual job, and if it's being advertised by a recruiter, it's more than likely that the job doesn't even exist!

If you're a manager, perception is everything. It's possible to make the worst job in the world look like a once-in-a-lifetime, not-to-be-missed opportunity if you paint the right picture and sell it effectively. Job descriptions are powerful opportunities to pull one over on potential employees and keep existing employees in a kind of confused limbo – use them well.

AUTHOR'S TIP:

Read job descriptions frequently to hone your skills. If they contain more than twenty words, you're probably reading something a recruitment consultant or HRM half-wit has spent days, if not *months, concocting. Churchill once wrote at the end of a ten-page letter to a friend, 'I would have written you a shorter letter but didn't have time.' BEWARE OF LONG JOB DESCRIPTIONS!*

CHAPTER 11: K IS FOR KITE-MARK, THE SYMBOL OF QUALITY

Quality is probably one of the most important but most frequently abused areas of management. Like beauty or the taste of salt, it's almost impossible to define so it's the *nirvana of bullshit management.*

In Ireland, the Culliton report highlights the need to put a cohesive and wide-ranging set of policy measures into place, through which Ireland's commercial and industrial base might be better equipped to create additional employment and wealth. By implication, the report emphasises the importance of achieving a more competitive environment and expresses a matching concern for the quality of products and services delivered to the marketplace, both at home and abroad.

For years management talked of 'quality this' and 'quality that' and employees eventually got fed up with their agenda-laden mantra – enter total quality management (TQM), an even more nebulous term. TQM was described by management as the next stage of our human evolution. Like every other area of management there's nothing magical or mystical about TQM – it's simply the application of common sense in a structured and formal way.

As human beings we're actually programmed to continually improve as part of the greater evolutionary process. If people were simply allowed to do their job to output requirements and expectations agreed beforehand, they would do it and do it better than with some foolish manager standing over them, consumed with the exuberance of his own verbosity.

Author's Tip:

If your organisation is big enough to have middle management, reduce your overheads considerably by removing them. Costs will decrease, quality will improve and the organisational BQ (bullshit quotient) will reduce dramatically. Try it out, it really works and it's fun!

With middle management out of the way there's a real possibility that quality will become a reality within your organisation.

There's a plethora of certified registered quality systems, ranging from the 'Q' mark to ISO9000-2000 (formerly the Kite-mark), EFQM modelling, HACCP, GMP, cGMP, ISO14001, etc., etc. The list is endless and very boring. If you're reasonably happy with the product of service you supply and, more importantly, if your customer is happy with the quality you provide, *there's nothing stopping you from advertising quality standards, even if you don't officially have them!* Take the last four digits of your mobile phone and make that your official registered firm status number – who's going to check it?

If like many Irish organisations, however, you feel compelled to obtain ISO9000-2000, then, like interviewing, it's easy. Simply take your existing business plan, renumber the paragraphs as per the ISO standard and write procedures for everything you can think off: how to answer the phone, how to process an order, how to train a human resource, how to handle a customer complaint, how to buy materials and services, how to maintain equipment, etc., etc. – let the creativity flow big time.

When you have about 100 procedures, you're on the home stretch. Next you'll need to contact the audit authorities and request a date for them to come and audit your efforts. They'll generally find fifteen to twenty non-conformances or issues for you to address, give you your framed ISO certificate of excellence and it's the last you'll see of them for six months. You will now be registered to an international quality management system!

When they come back in six months' time to review your progress, simply rewrite all the procedures the day before they arrive. They'll be pulling their hair out trying to wade through all the new bullshit procedures and before you know it, their two-day allotment to your company will be over. They'll have to move on to their next company, leaving you with another fifteen to twenty non-conformances to address. Six months later, simply rewrite all the procedures again – again they'll be pulling their hair out in frustration – guaranteed!

AUTHOR'S TIP:

If you haven't got the general wherewithal to continually keep pulling one over the auditors or solicitors have notified you to cease advertising quality standards you don't have, JUST MAKE UP YOUR *OWN QUALITY STANDARD. Use a combination of Greek letters and numbers like Sigma 28K, Omega-12B Model or QP-DAT-75000 Protocol.* Who's to know it's really a load of horseshit, *and you can rest assured that none of your competitors will have this standard!*

Hi-Impact Management Clichés

Some really good quality management clichés are 'quality is free', 'quality is everyone's business' and 'quality is management food'. These generic clichés can be dropped into almost every management situation.

When an employee says, 'I do my work and mind my own business, now get the hell away from me with that video camera, I've got rights', respond with, 'Quality is everyone's business'. Or if a different employee says, 'It's going to take me longer to do that and inspect it as well, it's going to cost you, I ain't doing extra work for free', respond with, 'Quality is free'.

The next time you're perusing the canteen dinner menu, ask the cook, 'How come quality isn't on the menu?' Tell the cook and everyone around you in the queue that you're simply amazed that it's not on the menu because 'quality is the very food of management'. It sends out the right message and lets everyone around you know YOU'RE A MANAGER.

CHAPTER 12: L IS FOR LUDDITES

Luddites were members of a band of English artisans who rioted against mechanisation and destroyed industrial machinery in the years 1811 to 1816. They were opposed to industrialisation and new technology and believed more would be lost than gained through it.

Though they received much bad press at the start of the industrial revolution, they do deserve a mention in all good management books (*as well as works of literary genius like this*). They felt that bunching people together and applying pre-scientific management theory on them was not such a good thing. They were right, in a strange sort of way.

In the Epinephrine trials of the 1950s, a workforce of 100 employees was divided into two equal sections. One half was pumped with Epinephrine and the other half with a placebo. They were then observed by management. Productivity from the spaced-out half was more than double that of the other half. Final management conclusions were inconclusive.

More conclusive were the infamous Hawthorn Studies carried out at the US Hawthorn Electric plant to examine the effect of working conditions on employee motivation. Employees were exposed to heat, cold, lack of food and water, electric shocks, verbal abuse, buckets of water thrown over them, varying lighting levels, etc.

One day management would turn down the temperature of the

working environment to below freezing and observe employees' 'motivation' through changes in productivity (a motivated employee is a productive employee). On another day management switched off all the lights and had employees work totally in the dark. To management's amazement, productivity increased each time a change was made to the working environment. Even when employees were observed in fridge-like working conditions, void of light, food and water and exposed to constant small but painful electric shocks, their productivity continued to increase! It was one of those 'eureka' moments for management – they could do nothing wrong and productivity (therefore motivation) just kept on increasing! Employees were eventually tethered to a post in the freezing dark and still gave increases in productivity. It was a major breakthrough for management theory.

AUTHOR'S TIP:
Vary your employees' working conditions and see what happens – run your own Hawthorn experiment – it's fun and educational.

It was only years later when other management theorists revisited the research data that they truly realised what was happening. Employees were not reaching dizzy heights of productivity (motivation) because management was screwing around with their minds, but rather because they were receiving some 'recognition' from management. This is now commonly known as the Hawthorn effect in management and is appropriate in commenting on a variety of situations. For example, 'Oh yeah, that's the Hawthorn effect', 'That seems a little Hawthornian to me', or 'It's clearly Hawthornish'.

In Ireland in 2001, a similar experiment to Hawthorn was carried out at an ESB power generation station in County Offaly. In this experiment, management investigated what would happen if they actually took the work away from the employees and ceased all production at the site. The company had previously supplied electricity to the national grid through a peat-fired process, but for the purpose of management research that would stop.

ALL EMPLOYEES WOULD RETAIN FULL PAY, BENEFITS, ETC.
Despite having nothing to do for eighteen months, all employees turned up for work, on time, every day. Management conclusions were less conclusive than with the Hawthorn studies. Employees would not leave the site. The management offered each and every one of them € 250,000.00 as a sweetener to leave the site but they were looking for more.

CONCLUSIONS: the management of the station are due to have cranial-rectal surgery before they can definitively establish:

1. What the hell was going on?
2. What lessons can they learn from the whole experiment?
3. Whether or not it's possible for management to manage a workforce when it's got its head firmly locked up its own ass.

The Luddites were a little extreme and had they been successful, we wouldn't have the mass-produced consumer goods we have now, nor would we have the groundbreaking management research of Hawthorn and the ESB.

Just as well their reign was cut short!

CHAPTER 13: M IS FOR MANAGEMENT

Sometimes described as grotesque, unseen, bizarre, unprecedented or rotten to the core, management is a general catch-all sort of concept.

If you've got good management you've got a good company, and if you've got bad management you've got a bad company. Management does it all – it built the pyramids, the Panama Canal, the *Titanic* and the Tower of Bullshit we call human resource management.

The best way to discover and tap into the art of management is to pick up one of those new small series management books. You'll find them at airport shops and airport executive toilet cubicles. Two excellent high-impact gems of books are *How to Fumble your Way through Business and Management* by Parson Butt and Keith Robinson or *Release the Crap from Within* by Dr Claude Voooon Hoote.

If you're good at bullshitting you'd probably make a good middle manager or recruitment consultant. Learn the principals of a good four-box window management model and throw them into conversation whenever possible (See Figure M1 overleaf).

While people are trying to figure out what the hell you're talking about, move the conversation swiftly along to some subject you feel comfortable bullshitting about – the weather, current affairs, etc.

Even if you yourself cannot bullshit, you can always hire someone to bullshit *on your behalf*. Delegation can be dangerous, but given with an element of fear it works well most of the time.

FIGURE M1: A GOOD FOUR-BOX MANAGEMENT WINDOW MODEL

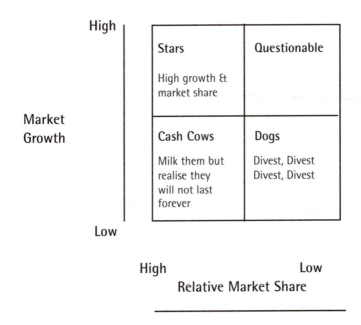

When having a morning coffee with an employee, mention a former employment of yours where you fired people on a regular basis just for the hell of it. Then rapidly change the conversation back to something more acceptable (weather, current affairs, the company's mission statement, etc.).

No book on management would be complete without some mention of acronym, cliché and buzzword. Read a few annual reports and you'll pick up a few gems of the more common space fillers – TQM, JIT, EFQM, TGIF, 'I've no axe to grind', 'People are our greatest asset', 'Quality is everyone's business', 'You've got to crack eggs to make an omelette', etc., etc.

Talk to a real-life management consultant if you want to establish an actual fluency in management acronym, cliché and buzz-words. Some consultants offer a complete or total package based on a high-impact weekend basis. The cost is around € 2000 but you'll get it back, AND MORE, in government training grants.

Some participating managers gave the following feedback from their high-impact learning weekend with Consultants 'R' Us, based in Slough, London:

I paid two grand for the weekend but had my accountant process a claim for three grand plus. I'd recommend it to all would-be managers.
Mr S. Gormley, Belfast

I enjoyed the weekend tremendously. On immediate return to work I baffled at least twenty people with my new-found fluency in the first hour of return! They didn't have a clue what I was talking about and neither did I – it was first class and I made a profit from the training grant!
Mr Buck I., Boise, Idaho

I loved the weekend and now never miss an opportunity to use my new art. I strike up a conversation with the wife, post-man, friends and work colleagues and then just turn on the crap-talk. I can waffle and bullshit on virtually every subject under the sun. Those consultants transformed my life.
Mr Willie U. Ryan, Santa Ponsa, Spain

The feedback and comments speak volumes. There's no better way to hone your management skills than a high-impact weekend approach. The cost includes lecture fees, notes, role play, paintball, psychometric testing, a full-body massage and as much alcohol as you can hold down in a sauna.

Another great method to brush up on your management skills is through networking with other managers outside of your own organisation. Management consultants will nearly always recommend managers' bingo for networking managers.

Using the card following, in Figure M2, check off each block when you hear the words during a meeting, seminar or phone call. When you get five blocks horizontally, vertically or diagonally, shout, 'Bullshit!' You'll not only update your own management jargon vocabulary, you'll also show those around you that you recognise all the words and are management savvy.

FIGURE M2

Synergy	Strategic fit	Core competencies	Best practice	Bottom line
revisit	take that offline	24/7	out of the loop	benchmark
value-added	Proactive	win–win	think outside	fast track
result-driven	empower or empowerment	knowledge base	at the end of the day	touch base
mindset	client focus(ed)	ballpark	game plan	leverage

Networking Managers' Bingo – Testimonials from Satisfied Players:

I had only been in the meeting for five minutes when I won. I've increased my management vocabulary three-fold from the exercise. I can barely speak English but am now fluent in management and talk it twenty-four seven, fifty-two.
Mr Sean Summers, Cape Cod, USA

My attention span at meetings has improved dramatically. I'm now awake and sober for 80 per cent of meetings.
Mr Buck I., Boise, Idaho

What a riot – food for thought – I was thrilled. Meetings will never be the same for me after my first win. With the stuff I learned, I now talk management jargon not only at work, but at home, with the kids and at the supermarket.
Dr Cod, Crawley, London

The atmosphere was tense in the last managers' meeting as fourteen of us waited for the fifth box – I nearly shat myself when I was the first to yell BULLSHIT!
Mr S. Gormley, Belfast

MIXED MANAGEMENT METAPHORS

In management you can get away with mixing up metaphors that don't make an ounce of sense. Most people will think it's some new management fad and one they're unfamiliar with, and they won't admit ignorance to something they're unfamiliar with.

For example, saying, 'We've really got to burst that lemming open' will bring a look of confusion to most people's faces. They'll know there's something about lemmings that they should be familiar with, but what? Or try, 'That vendor is too big to fry, let's poach the company in its own butter.' This makes no sense whatsoever but perhaps it's a new concept in vendor or supply chain management theory? Or how about, 'Yeah, it's the 'magnified posse' phenomenon, you know.' The only limit is your own creativity and ability to bullshit with confidence!

Once you've got the talk, get the walk and combine. The walk should be fast, ass-clenching, purposeful, strong and energetic with a hint of mystery. Always aloof, but always ducking and diving as threats and opportunities arise.

Chapter 14: N is for Never and Make it Forever

Never, ever admit you were wrong in management. A glass eye in a duck's ass may see you're as guilty as sin, but never, never admit being wrong. Blame the situation, the environment, other people, customers, suppliers – blame anything but yourself.

Author's Tip:

Procrastinate – delay, drag your heels and buy yourself some time. Then just think up a load of bullshit that sounds credible in some way. If you admit that you were ever wrong, you'll show  *weakness and invoke a mutiny. Mutinies are only good when you're the manager co-ordinating the project.*

Procrastination is the very cornerstone of good management practice.

Fight your corner and never admit being wrong.

CHAPTER 15: O IS FOR OFFICE

The office is an extension of your personality and should ooze the same confidence that permeates you and your daily activities as a manager.

The bigger the desk, the more important you feel so get the biggest one possible. If you can't physically fit your new desk into the office, have it actually built inside the office – banquet-sized! The same goes for the chair – get something high backed and throne like. Place all your degrees, diplomas and industry achievement awards directly behind your throne. Literally wallpaper the place with loads of wonderful things about yourself – don't hold back. (On my own wall I keep my driving certificate of competence amongst hundreds of other things).

You'll probably be spending a fair amount of time in the office so make sure it's well equipped from the start. Get a good coffee machine, an ashtray, a calculator, jacuzzi, a TV, a remote control and a telephone. The telephone should allow you to take and make conference calls while watching TV in the jacuzzi.

Always keep your huge desk immaculately clean. A clean desk is the very hallmark of a good leader. When good leaders place something in the middle of their huge desk people instinctively know it's important.

For the first few weeks in your new office, go in really early in the morning. Aim to be at your desk and in your throne at six am every morning. Then, have your secretary/PA go in every morning, open the office, switch things on and make it look like you're actually there.

You'll be able to swan off for the day while your employees and colleagues will perceive you to be working away big time. Keep the employees on their toes by occasionally sleeping in the office. There's an array of executive sleeping bags at most good camping stores.

Your office is a powerful and highly visible symbol of your greatness as a manager. If business is booming, get a bigger office, more furniture, a shower, a foot spa, a fridge, an apartment. Don't be afraid to spend cash – your office should literally smell of money and success.

If there's a communal canteen at work, make sure the table you visit for lunch is slightly higher than all the others. Two or three inches will do the job and let people know you're management, you're great and you're superior. Chairs, too, should reflect your managerial status – high-backed leather ones make a statement in the canteen. If the canteen is a buffet-like scenario, have the canteen manager come to your table like a waitress and take your order. Management shouldn't have to stand in line with everyone else. Even when you're in the canteen, carry loads of files and paperwork with you and talk about nothing except work, the mission statement and your management vision (See Chapter 22: Vision) for the future.

Generally speaking, looking busy is always more effective than being busy (and also more fun). The amount of paper you carry around all day is directly proportional to the impression of your pretended caseload.

OUTSOURCING

Outsourcing is simply taking some part of your business you're either fed up trying to fix or can't be bothered dealing with, giving it to someone else and letting them do it. The need to outsource comes about as organisations get fat, slow and unresponsive to their customers and market. You can survive being fat and slow but eventually you may need to outsource something.

Reverse integration is the opposite of outsourcing, where you take the business back into your own organisation because the company doing the outsourcing gets fat, slow and unresponsive. It's a continuous cycle of outsource, reverse integrate, outsource, reverse integrate, etc.

AUTHOR'S TIP:

Outsource all non-strategic functions of your business, such as canteen catering, car park mainte-nance and HR management. When you see and *understand how the outsource company does the function better, integrate it (take it back) into your business – except for HRM. Just ignore HRM once you've outsourced it and eventually it will disappear.*

CHAPTER 16: P IS FOR PETER PRINCIPLE

The Peter Principle was first introduced by L. Peter in a humour book (of the same title) describing the pitfalls of bureaucratic organisations. The original principle states that in a hierarchically structured administration, people tend to be promoted up to their level of incompetence. The Civil Service gives us excellent examples of incompetence and the Peter Principle is based on the observation that in such an organisation new employees typically start in the lower ranks, but when they prove to be competent in the task to which they are assigned, they get promoted to a higher rank. This process of climbing up the hierarchical ladder can go on indefinitely until the employee reaches a position where he or she is no longer competent. At that moment the process typically stops, since the established rules of bureaucracies make it very difficult to demote someone to a lower rank (a job for life), even if that person would be much better fitted and more happy in that lower position. The net result is that most of the higher levels of a bureaucracy will be filled by incompetent people who got there because they were quite good at doing a different (and usually, but not always, easier) task than the one they are now expected to do.

The evolutionary generalisation of the Principle is less pessimistic in its implications, since evolution lacks the bureaucratic inertia that pushes and maintains people in an unfit position.

But what will certainly remain is that systems confronted by evolutionary problems will quickly tackle the easy ones, but tend to get stuck in the difficult ones. The better a system is (more fit, smarter, more competent, more adaptive) the more quickly it will solve all the easy problems, but a more difficult problem will be what it finally gets stuck in. Getting stuck here doesn't mean being unfit, it just means reaching the limit of one's competence and thus having great difficulty advancing further. This explains why even the most complex and adaptive species, such as ourselves, humans, are always still struggling for survival in their niches as energetically as the most primitive organisms, such as bacteria. If ever a species were to get control over all its evolutionary problems, more complex problems would arise so that the species would continue to balance on the border of its domain of incompetence. In conclusion, the generalised Peter Principle states that in evolution, systems tend to develop up to the limit of their adaptive competence.

The Peter Principle is more than management theory and can be seen in many organisations. It's not limited to bureaucratic hierarchies and always appears friggin' obvious after the event.

Take the case of one large American pharmaceutical company with headquarters in Dublin and previously headed up by dodgy accountants. Each financial quarter, the company delivered sparkling results and it just kept getting better and better. But one of the things fuelling this apparent growth was the creation of 'off balance sheet entities and complex joint ventures'. Funds would 'leave' the company and then 'return' to the company boosting its bank balance situation – some fancy financial footwork. Everyone was aware of funds coming into the company but nobody noticed the fact that these were the SAME FUNDS leaving it. It was a type of boomerang operation and it worked beautifully.

If it weren't for the mighty Enron Corporation going belly up, a spate of other accounting shenanigans and a little too much use of the boomerang, the company would still be delivering sparkling (though complete bullshit) results each quarter. It looked like it was going to go bust but a frantic fire sale appears to have saved its ass. Needless to say, the two dancing accountants were frog-marched the hell out of there!

Eircom is the national telephone service provider in Ireland. In the great Eircom share flop, the whole country got involved. The

Non-factored risk.

prospectus from Eircom for the largest single Irish initial public offering (IPO) was released at the end of a phenomenal bull market, when everyone thought there was only one way for shares to go – up. The prospectus detailed four very carefully written (cover-your-ass) pages of risk factors and every one of them turned out to be legitimate warnings. It all looked clear enough and was affording the general public an opportunity to jump on the stocks and shares bandwagon. However, the additional risk, not mentioned in the prospectus, was that management might not be able to steer the company out of trouble, if trouble came via non-factored risk. Sounds like Peter! Trouble came, everyone holding Eircom shares got burned and the cause of the Irish stock-owning democracy was set back for a long, long time. Since then a number of IPOs have been pulled at the last minute. Once burned – twice shy.

Banking in Ireland has provided some great examples of the Peter Principle. For instance, take one Irish bank's interests in America and the young currency dealer, Mr John Ransack. John told his superiors he could make a lot of money running numbers. He could run a large option book hedged in the cash markets. The bankers quickly hired him and for years John was an indispensable part of the treasury dealing team.

He seemed to be doing exactly what he had promised, but nobody was checking his books! He was actually perpetrating the fourth-largest currency fraud in history and lost the bank $691,000,000.00! The bank had to sell loads of stuff in the US to claw back some money and some face. It all appeared friggin' obvious after the event.

The very same bank nearly went belly up back in 1985 when it contested a bid for the Insurance Corporation of Ireland and decided to forget about DUE DILIGENCE. The bank must have known what it was doing and seemd to have ignored the basics of accountancy. Ignoring the basics is like trying to drive a car blindfolded and knowing it contains 100 pounds of Semtex connected to a mercury switch – it's dangerous. The bank boss got out of there pretty fast when he realised what the hell was going on but not before the State had to be called to perform a rescue operation. The total cost of the failure was about $511,000,000.00 and shareholders paid for about 80 per cent. The financial auditors were sued and contributed about eighteen per cent of costs.

However, banks are very powerful and it's not a good idea to remind them of their lost battles – get on the right side of them and you're laughing. They can provide bogus accounts, false international addresses, assumed identities and tax avoidance schemes the mafia would be proud to use. USE BANKS TO YOUR ADVANTAGE.

Author's Tip:

Be aware of the Peter Principle – it exists in what looks like the best-managed companies on the face of the planet. If you're aware of it as a manager, you'll never be caught out by it. Consider a bogus account, false identity and address abroad before that sort of thing is outlawed. It might be your last chance to avoid a little tax! Even Government Minister's do it!

CHAPTER 17: Q IS FOR QUANTITATIVE TECHNIQUES OR STATISTICS

There are lies, damned lies and statistics, or so wrote Benjamin Disraeli – or was it Mark Twain? Whoever it was, he was right and you can be 100 per cent sure of that. Quantitative techniques or statistics is the only science that enables different experts using the exact same figures to draw dramatically different conclusions. The practitioner of statistics, or statistician, can go directly from an unwarranted assumption to a preconceived conclusion. They believe that figures under analysis don't lie but sometimes they don't stand up, either. Brilliant with numbers, statisticians fall short of the personality threshold to become an accountant. Many will cite the practical application of statistics back to the beginning of time itself, but it was really born as a science in 1654 when a French nobleman asked a famous mathematician, Blaise Pascal, to solve a gambling problem – *namely, how to win!*

As a management tool, STATISTICS CAN MAKE HEAVEN LOOK LIKE HELL AND HELL LOOK LIKE PARADISE. Within this understanding lies MANAGEMENT OPPORTUNITY – a fundamental appreciation of statistics allows the manager to bullshit on virtually every subject.

For example, that *30 per cent of all printing companies will disappear in the next five years* was a statistical prediction in 2003. It's right and it's wrong but it has the potential to scare. Apocalyptic predictors would like to think it's right, as they've been predicting the death of the written word since it first gave joy to our species.

Telephones were supposed to render the written word redundant, as was radio, television, photocopiers, fax machines, computers, personal digital assistants and, more recently, the internet.

On the other hand, if print companies were to offer services other than providing the printed word (i.e., packaging their customers' products along with their print or distributing their print on behalf of the customer), they could cease to be a printer and evolve to become a service provider. This being the case, even more than 30 per cent of print companies would disappear, but would there be a reciprocal 30 per cent increase in companies providing services which include print? This is a fundamental law in physics – to each and every action there is an opposite reaction, what goes up must come down, etc., etc.

Whether it's 30 per cent here or 30 per cent there, as a manager you've got to *remember that it's statistics*, it's interpretation and under intellectual scrutiny, *it's bullshit*. Prophets of doom have always existed and always will and statistics will always provide justification for their existence.

Senior management and politicians can be observed tactically using statistics on a daily basis. When cornered and when rational and irrational argument fails – when there is nowhere left to turn – QUOTE STATISTICS. THEY WILL SAVE THE DAY. Additionally, the manager may use statistics as a last-ditch strategy to influence, distort and confirm his power base. For example, management set the following targets/key performance indicators (KPIs):

- *KPI 1:* cost:revenue ratio must reach 10 per cent.
- *KPI 2:* warehouse stock/inventory must turn 26 times per year or every two weeks.

- *KPI 3:* service delivery performance must be 99 per cent of all orders in less than five working days.

After chasing these targets for a year, training the workforce, applying participative management, examining and rightsizing, benchmarking and using world-class manufacturing application and balanced scorecard techniques, he finally hits all three targets – simultaneously and at the same time. What next? He's reached all his KPIs and his workforce has arrived at the end of their targeted journey. This is where statistics enter the equation, coupled with a dollop of waffle.

It's true, we've improved our cost/revenue ratio, slashed the amount of stock we have in our warehouse and improved our customer rating considerably, but ...

STATISTICS SHOW:
- Our market is experiencing negative exponential growth share.
- Our customers have reset the goalposts and realigned their expectations.
- Our competitors are not playing to the same rules nor playing with the same ball.
- Our suppliers are in bed with the competition and they ain't plucking turkey.
- The moon could fall to earth.
- Aliens could make a bid for our markets share.
- Our industry is expecting a 30 per cent sectored amputation over the next five years due to forces above and beyond normal buyer attrition and evolving purchasing power.

IN SUMMARY, IT'S STATISTICALLY PREDICTED THAT 30 PER CENT OF PRINTING COMPANIES WILL DISAPPEAR IN THE NEXT FIVE YEARS!

AUTHOR'S TIP:

Learn the basics about statistics and RECOGNISE THE TRUE BULLSHIT POTENTIAL OF THIS SCIENCE – it is sim- *ply phenomenal! Recognise in conversation that when the word percentage is uttered, it's generally a prelude to bullshit from the person speaking.*

CHAPTER 18: R IS FOR RECRUITMENT CONSULTANT

In the booming Irish Celtic Tiger economy of the late 1990s, hiring people was virtually impossible. Unemployment reached its lowest rate ever and the number of recruitment companies in Ireland reached its peak at over 800 – phenomenal growth.

With no market entry barriers other than € 500, a clean criminal record and the ability to string five or six paragraphs together in a semi-coherent job description (see Chapter 10: Job Description), it's understandable that many would enter the recruitment market. Even traditional and socially challenged accountancy firms saw the massive potential and started building up databases of human resources and human resource buyers.

However, there's an inverse (and perverse) relationship between quantity and quality. When quantity is high, quality is low and vice versa – it's a kind of universal balancing thing. As the number of feeding recruiters increased, the pie (market share) they were feeding on decreased.

In attempts to maintain growth and market share (remember the four-window grid, Figure M1), many recruiters developed shady business practices, such as:

1. Back-hole filling. Here the recruiter would place the same person in fifteen different companies in the same year, back-hole filling (as it's called) the fourteen new available positions. The frequent mover has upped his earnings and gained a few insights along the way, the company has a new human resource and the recruiter is getting plastered drunk in a hotel penthouse jacuzzi.

2. Weeding and feeding protocol. Here the recruiter would convince an unsuspecting employed person to resign from their current position on the basis that they had a better position on offer. Once the person resigned (weed), the recruiter would run into the company with a load of CVs to save the day and fill the position (feed). The person who was previously employed but resigned doesn't come off too well here.

3. Scratching and matching protocol. Although less common than the first two practices, scratching and matching is found frequently in Limerick. In this practice, the recruiter will start by getting to know a little information about the target. The target will be the person intended for the 'scratch'. Once they've established what the target's job is, their salary, who they report to and who reports to them (target's job description), they'll scratch the target. This involves following them, bundling them into the back of a van and holding them at an isolated location long enough for their position to become vacant. Once the position becomes vacant, they'll contact the company and 'match' the position with a plethora of CVs and candidates. When they've been paid for their service in filling the position, they'll release the captive, usually still blindfolded and cuffed, close to the location they were picked up from.

Recruitment is one of those self-regulating industries, so ethics is an optional extra and you can bill your clients for *anything* extra! Morals are wall paintings and a scruple is the currency of Russia.

There are some professional recruitment companies out there and it's worth pointing out that it's only the majority of them that are dodgy.

It's what a lot of American business people would call a 'no-brainer', but all good things must come to an end and the post-Celtic Tiger year of 2002 saw 200 recruitment companies close.

Like the salesman with the magical elixir, chocolate-flavoured cheese and the TV repair engineer, it's a market niche unprotected by the unrelenting bombardment of time and common sense.

What goes around comes around, fly too close to the sun and you'll get your ass burned, make hay while the sun shines – all great clichés, and as always in management, always appropriate.

If your business goes belly up and you're obliged to deal with recruitment consultants, there are ten common pitfalls. Forewarned is forearmed:

1. They phone you up saying that they have several jobs that you are suitable for. However, they first need you to supply them with references. Is this true? No, it isn't. They don't have any jobs for you. They are just trying to find people who take on people and want to know the names and phone numbers of your old bosses. Don't trust the bastards.

2. They'll say, 'Who did you work for at company XYZ? Was it Graham Sutherland?' 'No,' you say. 'It was John Salisbury.' Now they have a contact at your old firm. They'll find out where John Salisbury lives, where he shops and where he socialises and through stalking him they'll eventually get to ask him if he's looking for any CVs.

3. They post jobs on job boards that don't exist. They are only trying

to get themselves a number of extra CVs to increase their own database. When you send in your CV, they'll say that the job is gone.

4. They'll ask you, 'Tell us what companies your CV has already been sent out to so that we don't make the mistake of sending your CV there again, which could cost you a job interview.' If you tell them, they now know what companies are looking for candidates and they can then put some other candidates up in opposition to you. Don't think they wouldn't!

5. When they are asking you what your remuneration for the job is they might say, 'What's your bottom line? What's the least that you would take to get a job? Obviously we will try to get as much as we can for you.' No they won't. Your bottom line now becomes the most you'll get for any job. They'll still try and get as much as they can from the client, but they'll keep any extra they can get for themselves. How many people have actually heard a recruiter say, 'We've managed to get you a higher rate than you were asking for'?

6. They'll put a clause in your contract that they and the client company can terminate you with a month's (or a week's) notice, but that you have no notice period with them. Always read the small print.

7. If you get a job interview through them, they'll tell you that they'll call you back when they have any news. What they mean is that if there's good news, they'll be on the line pronto to try and get you to sign up straightaway in case you take another job. If it's bad news, they won't call you and they won't be around when you drop in. They'll give you the bad news eventually, but only after several attempts to get hold of them. They'll suggest your e-mail isn't working, your phone was engaged or they requested some-

one else to call you days earlier. If you don't get the job for an interview that they sent you to, they'll say they'll look for other jobs for you, but they won't. They'll quietly drop you. They don't like people who don't pass interviews for them.

9. They tell you that if you introduce them to another candidate who they get a job for, they'll pay you. They will if you find out about it. They won't contact you unless you call up asking for it and even then they'll attempt to deny everything. If they get this person a job three months down the line or a couple of years down the line, there's no chance at all of them sending you payment, despite the fact that the finder's name (yours) will be on their database.

10. Once they've got you a job, they may say that they weren't able to get you the salary that you wanted – but that the client will only pay five per cent or ten per cent less. *This is bullshit.* They told the company what your salary was initially and the company accepted it. The agency is now just trying to help themselves to an extra bit of cash for a job that is safely in their pockets. Don't fall for it. Tell them that their client can shove the friggin' job up the high hole of their ass and see how quickly they change track. They don't want to lose sure-fire money.

AUTHOR'S TIP:

Avoid recruitment companies like the plague – they're not all dodgy but for € 100 the vast majority would sell their own granny! If you send *your details to a recruiter,* understand that it will be viewed by many people and may be used as filler material when they're submitting a bunch of CVs to a particular company.

Chapter 19: S is for Service Management

Whether your business is supplying goods or services, there will always be some element of service management. Customers, like cars, must be regularly serviced. Increasing customer service quality will increase customer satisfaction, leading to higher sales, higher profits, a bigger office and bigger car. Indeed, it has been shown that companies that are rated highly on service quality perform better in terms of market share, growth and profitability.

However, many large companies and semi-state companies fail to understand the whole service quality concept. To them, service quality remains an elusive goal. There are four root causes of poor perceived service quality and these are the barriers that separate the perceptions of service quality from what customers expect, want and receive.

1. The misconceptions barrier. This arises from management's misunderstanding of what the customer actually expects. Lack of market research or common sense may lead managers to misconceive the important service attributes that customers use in service evaluation.

For example, a restaurant manager may believe that shortening the gaps between courses may improve customer satisfaction, when the customer actually values a pause between eating. On a larger scale, management of the national railway may believe that customers actually enjoy standing for three to four hours on a 150-mile trip from Dublin to Cork without basic catering facilities but with portaloo toilets, befowled by excrement. Good market and customer research will demonstrate they don't!

2. Inadequate resources barrier. Management may understand customer expectations but be unwilling to provide the resources to meet them. This may arise because of a cost reduction measure, a productivity focus or simply because management are clowns.

3. Inadequate delivery barrier. Managers may understand customer expectations and supply adequate resources to meet those expectations but fail to select, train and reward staff adequately. This results in poor or inconsistent service delivery and may manifest itself in poor communication skills, inappropriate dress, unwillingness to solve customer problems or a fist fight.

4. Exaggerated promises barrier. Even when management understands what customers want and have adequate and trained human resources in place, there can still be a gap between customer expectations and perceptions. Advertising and sales messages that build expectations to a pitch that cannot be fulfilled may leave customers disappointed. For example, a hotel brochure that claims a hotel is only a ten-minute stroll through a trendy boulevard to the sea when the hotel is in Mullingar is almost guaranteed to disappoint. Mullingar is in the midlands, nowhere near the sea, and is where they'd put the pipe in if the country needed an enema.

Similarly, if you're working in retail management and are advising customers that they'll 'get their hole' if they buy a particular suit, be prepared for possible repercussions. Disgruntled customers may be coming back to your shop a week later, dissatisfied with the product and looking for a cash refund. Don't over-exaggerate your product or service offering.

Author's Tip:
Go for some catchy yet non-committal slogan, like 'We're not there yet but we're getting there', or 'A lot done, more to do'.

If you don't define where you're actually going or what you actually intend to do, who's to say you haven't reached or even exceeded your goals?

In understanding customers' service expectations, the manager must understand the service attributes, or what makes a service good. According to Dr Claude Voooon Hoote, author and founding member of THCIMR (The Hackballs Cross Institute of Management Research), there are ten service attributes important to customers. These are worth learning by heart for coffee break or canteen conversation material:

1. The call-back. Always call the customer back when you promise to do so. It may be a ten-second call where all of a sudden you've got to take a call on another line or attend some (pretend) meeting, but always call them back. You can call them the next day when things have cooled down. Procrastination is the very cornerstone of service management.

2. The problem explanation. This doesn't necessarily have to be the truth as to what actually happened, just an explanation. It's an opportunity for the manager to bring in a bit of creative waffle, or if the customer isn't taking the bait, technical jargon. Blind them with technicality and once you notice large gaps of silence on the other end of the line, you'll know you're making progress.

3. The contact number. Customers will always ask who they can talk to in order to have the problem resolved. The number you provide doesn't necessarily have to be the CORRECT NUMBER. It could be the number of someone in the human resources department, who more than likely is just sitting around scratching themself. Give them something to do and get yourself off the hook – let them talk with the customer. The important thing is for you to provide a contact number.

4. Prompt contact. Call the customer as soon as you realise there's a major cock-up. If you get really good at this you can call them before they actually perceive the problem, lower their expectations and eliminate the issue before it becomes a complaint.

5. Resolution time frame. Give customers a 48-hour deadline – you can always call them before the deadline is up and extend the time frame indefinitely. By calling them before the deadline ends, they'll perceive the situation as being acted on and resolved. Eventually they'll stop asking for finite resolution as other problems take centre stage.

7. Alternative resolutions. These alternatives may be totally impractical, unworkable and outrageous, but mixed with a dollop of management buzzwords, technical jargon and basic waffle they will distract the customer from the initial complaint!

8. The person approach. You don't have to lather them up the ass, just treat them how you yourself would like to be treated.

9. Resolution to prevent another/future occurrence. Tell them you'll be holding a meeting with all the relevant management and if necessary, heads will roll and downsizing will follow. Eventually the customer will feel guilty at the thought of someone losing their job and the problem is diluted or may even disappear.

10. The progress report. If you've got no progress to report, make some up. It could be a big-time meeting with senior management in attendance or an ongoing staff appraisal of the people associated with the complaint. Tell them HR are involved and no stone will be left unturned, no river too deep, no mountain too high – you will provide total resolution, organisation-wide resolution, resolution on a scale unheard of before!

SERVICE MANAGEMENT IS IMPORTANT IN AN IRISH MANAGEMENT CONTEXT and increasing in importance globally. Learn the basic service management skills and your customer base will be gagging for more of the same.

However, if you're a manager in a semi-state company, a monopoly or a bank, service to the customer doesn't really matter!

CHAPTER 20: T IS FOR TRAINING

No matter what you do in life, you'll need training. As humans, we learn a lot slower than other so-called lesser species on the planet but we take on more and live relatively longer. We're top of the old food chain.

However, when we're born we can't even wipe our own asses without direct adult supervision, effective management and years of training and practice.

As infants, we train at not defecating ourselves. With slow progress, we train at wearing pants, we train at walking and we train at talking. We train our mind through education, train our body to drive a car, train our accountants to keep the books clean and keep ourselves fit, healthy and active through daily physical training.

TRAINING IS AN IMPORTANT AND POWERFUL FORCE WITHIN ANY BUSINESS. It's unfortunate that so many organisations don't recognise the power they could unleash if they applied it effectively.

We've all heard stories of people working within organisations for years and years in some dark backroom of the factory, fed through a door slot, beaten frequently about the head, never seeing the light of day and never, ever receiving any basic training or opportunity to better themselves. If they were only pulled out and unleashed they would contribute so much more than they did the day before – guaranteed.

Cast your mind back to Chapter 5 – E is for Expansion – and the two most critical points in applying business strategy:

1. Not having the right people in place and
2. Not having people trained sufficiently.

This isn't rocket science and can be great fun.

Job Training Methods
There are many different ways to train. Indeed, entire books have been written on the ways to deliver training. How can a manager charged with training his or her employees choose an appropriate method?

The method by which training is delivered often varies based on the needs of the company, the trainee and on the task being performed. The method should suit the audience, the content, the business environment and the financial objective. Ideally, the method chosen will motivate employees to learn, help employees to prepare themselves for learning, enable the trainees to apply and practice what they've been taught, help trainees retain and transfer what they've learned and integrate performance with other skills and knowledge.

Other factors affecting the choice of a training method include:

* Age, gender or level of education of the trainees.
* Budget.
* Availability of state-sponsored grants.
* Investment versus financial return on investment.
* Whether or not you actually want a trained workforce.

Broadly, there are two types of training: group based and individual based. Some of the more common group training methods include the following.

1. Lecture. A lecture is the method learners most often commonly associate with college and secondary education. Yet it's also considered one of the least effective methods to use for adult learners. In this method, one person (the trainer) does all of the talking. He or she may use handouts, visual aids, mannequins, pantomime horses or posters to support the lecture. Communication is primarily one way, from the instructor to the learner. ONE-WAY COMMUNICATION ALWAYS WORKS BEST FOR MANAGEMENT.

Pros: less time is needed for the trainer to prepare than other methods. It provides a lot of information quickly when it's less important that the trainees retain a lot of details. It's a good opportunity for the manager to try out a little new bullshit on fresh unsuspecting employees and can help pump the ego.

Cons: does not actively involve trainees in training process. The trainees forget much information if it's presented only orally. To counteract this, have all participants provide a 10,000 word essay on the lecture, giving them 24 hours to complete it.

2. Demonstration. Demonstration is very effective for basic skills training. The trainer shows trainees how to do something. The trainer may provide an opportunity for trainees to perform the task, such as how to drive a bus.

Pros: this method emphasises trainee involvement. It engages the senses: seeing, hearing, feeling, smelling, touching.

Cons: it requires a great deal of trainer preparation and planning. There also needs to be an adequate space for the training to take place, especially if a full-scale bus is being used as a prop. If the trainer is not skilled in the task being taught, poor work habits can be learned by the trainee.

3. Seminar. Seminars often combine several group methods: lectures, discussions, conferences or demonstrations. A grand day out is generally had by all.

Pros: group members are involved in the training. The trainer can use many group methods as part of the seminar activity. Effective monkey-see-monkey-do behaviour is instilled in the trainee.

Cons: planning is time consuming. The trainer must have skill in conducting a seminar. More time is needed to conduct a seminar than is needed for many other methods. Money is lost by having people away from their work stations.

4. Conference. The conference training method is a good problem-solving approach. A group considers a specific problem or issue and they work to reach agreement on statements or solutions. This could be something along the lines of escaping from an erupting volcano with nothing but a piece of string, a box of matches and team skills.

Pros: there is a lot of trainee participation. The trainees build consensus and the trainer can use several methods (lecture, panel, seminar) to keep sessions interesting.

Cons: it can be difficult to control a group. Opinions generated at the conference may differ from the manager's ideas, causing conflict. The trainees could lodge an assault charge against the trainer if limbs are broken.

5. Panel. A panel provides several points of view on a topic to seek alternatives to a situation. Panel members may have differing views but they must also have objective concerns for the purpose of the training. This is an excellent method for using outside resource people, if you can get them cheap.

Pros: trainees often find it interesting to hear different points of view. The process invites employees to share their opinions and they are challenged to consider alternatives. No matter how stupid these alternatives are, the manager must be at least seen to listen.

Cons: it requires a great deal of preparation. The results of the method can be difficult to evaluate. The manager has to do a lot of listening. This can be extremely difficult for many managers.

6. Role playing. During a role play, the trainees assume roles and act out situations connected to the learning concepts. It's good for customer service and sales training, but not advised for training people in dealing with dangerous animals (lions, elephants, etc).

Pros: trainees can learn possible results of certain behaviours in a classroom situation. They get an opportunity to practice real-life people skills. It's possible to experiment with many different approaches to a situation without alienating any customers.

Cons: a lot of time is spent making a single point. Trainers must be skilled and creative in helping the class learn from the situation. In some role-play situations, only a few people get to practice while others watch. Some people in a role-play situation may start acting like morons.

7. Case Studies. A case study is a description of a real or imagined situation that contains information that trainees can use to analyse what has occurred and why. The trainees recommend solutions based on the content provided.

Pros: a case study can present a real-life situation that lets trainees consider what they would do. It can present a wide variety of skills in which applying knowledge is important. Trainees can be made to make the case study at home at their own cost, thereby saving training costs.

Cons: cases can be difficult to write and time consuming to discuss. The trainer must be creative and very skilled at leading discussions, making points and keeping trainees on track. This is all the more difficult if they're working from home.

8. Simulations. Trainees participate in a reality-based interactive activity where they imitate actions required on the job. It's a useful technique for skills development.

Pros: training becomes more reality based, as trainees are actively involved in the learning process. It directly applies to jobs performed after training. Simulations involve yet another learning style, increasing the chance that trainees will retain what they have learned. Trainees can practice at home with toy telephones, toy photocopiers and toy fax machines without causing damage to expensive equipment.

Cons: simulations are time consuming. The trainer must be very skilled and make sure that trainees practice the skills correctly. Only perfect practice makes perfect. Toy photocopiers can be hard to find and expensive.

9. Projects. Projects require the trainees to do something on the job that improves the business as well as helps them learn about the topic of training. It might involve participation on a team, the creation of a database or forming a new process. The type of project will vary between businesses and the skill level of the trainee.

Pros: this is a good training activity for experienced employees. Projects can be chosen that help solve problems or otherwise improve the operation. Trainees get first-hand experience in the topic of the training. Little time is needed to prepare the training experience and you'll get some expensive work done on the cheap.

Cons: without proper introduction to the project and its purpose, trainees may think they are doing somebody else's work. Also, if they don't have an interest in the project or there's no immediate impact on their own jobs, it will be difficult to obtain and maintain their interest. You may have to threaten dismissal to motivate them appropriately.

Individual training methods focus on the individual and some of the more common ones include:

1. Self-discovery. Trainees discover the competencies on their own using such techniques as guided exercises, books and research.

Pros: trainees are able to choose the learning style that works best for them. They are able to move at their own pace and have a great deal of ownership over their learning. *The manager can leave them to their own devices to discover their true self.*

Cons: trainees can easily get side tracked and may move more slowly than the trainer desires. It's also more difficult to measure the employee's progress. Giving some employees lots of space is not always a good idea. Left alone and unmanaged, some would rob the place blind and get out of there faster than you could shout, 'Call HRM!' This method doesn't suit all employees.

2. Movies/videos/computer-based training. Content for the training experience comes primarily from a videotape or computer-based programme.

Pros: it's easy to provide this training and the trainer can follow up with questions and discussion. It's also easy to assure that the same information is presented to each trainee. This training is excellent for lazy, couch-potato employees.

Cons: it's expensive to develop. Most trainers choosing this option must purchase the training from an outside vendor, making the content less specific to their needs. *Some employees will break the TV if they don't like what they're seeing.*

3. On-the-job training. This is the most common method of

training. The trainee is placed on the job and left to their own devices. To be successful, the training should be done according to a structured programme that uses task lists, job breakdowns and performance standards as a lesson plan. In the absence of these, just let the new employee figure it out. As they're new to the position, they won't want to create a fuss.

Pros: the training can be made extremely specific to the employee's needs. It's highly practical and reality based. It also helps the employee establish important relationships with his or her manager. A strong bond may develop.

Cons: training is not standardised for employees. There is often a tendency to have a person learn by doing the job, providing no real training. As a method, it's not suitable for airline pilots or bus drivers. It's not a good idea to bond too much – things can get awkward when firing them later on.

4. Mentoring. A mentor can tutor others in their learning. Mentors help employees solve problems both through training them in skills and through modelling effective attitudes and behaviours. This system is sometimes known as a buddy system.

Pros: it can take place before, during or after a shift. It gives the trainee individual attention and immediate feedback. It also helps the trainee get information regarding the business culture and organisational structure. It presents a good opportunity for the manager to yank off about all his previous business conquests and is healthy for building the manager's ego.

Cons: training can be interrupted if the mentor moves on. If a properly trained mentor is not chosen, the trainee can pick up bad habits. Similarly, *if the mentor is a scumbag, the employee may also become a scumbag.*

When choosing from among these methods, the trainer must  decide which one best suits the trainees, the environment and the budget available. Many trainers will choose to combine methods or vary them. Others will select a single method that works best for them and never vary.

Unlimited management creativity.

With so many options a trainer is limited only by his or her creativity, and a manager has no limits in that department.

CHAPTER 21: U IS FOR UNDERSTANDING MANAGEMENT LANGUAGE

At this stage of your journey you should be able to understand the language of management without thinking twice. It should be an intuitive instinct or second nature. Testing your understanding on a regular basis is of paramount importance to ensure you're always honing your new-found skills. Carry out the following scientific test at least twice a year to ensure you're always in tune with your intuition.

1. Read the following advertisements aloud to yourself and before you read the actual translations, try and figure out what the employer is looking for.

2. Once you've got an idea of what the employer is actually looking for, consult the translation that appears in italics and then give yourself a performance rating on how you performed. Performance ratings will be between one and five. A rating of one means you fully understood. *A rating of five means you didn't have a friggin' clue.*

3. Once you've reviewed all statements and filled in all performance ratings, add up your total score, multiply it by ten and then consult the Performance Score Rating Index.

This will provide a snapshot rating in relation to general

wherewithal and chosen career path.

---

1. COMPETITIVE SALARY.
We remain competitive by paying less than our competitors. Any salary is competitive if you're currently out of work.
Performance rating:

　　　1.　　2.　　3.　　4.　　5.

---

2. JOIN OUR FAST-PACED COMPANY.
We have no time to train you. You'll have to introduce yourself to your co-workers, find the toilets, clear your own space to work and place yourself on a steep learning curve.

Performance rating:

　　　1.　　2.　　3.　　4.　　5.

---

3. NATIONALLY RECOGNISED LEADER.
Some buck-eye regional newspaper wrote us up a few years ago, but we haven't done anything innovative since.

Performance rating:

　　　1.　　2.　　3.　　4.　　5.

---

4. IMMEDIATE OPENING.
The person who used to have this job gave their notice a month ago. Yesterday, management noticed the person wasn't here any longer and decided to run the ad.

Performance rating:

　　　1.　　2.　　3.　　4.　　5.

---

5. SALES POSITION REQUIRING MOTIVATED SELF-STARTER.
We're not going to supply you with training, there's no base salary and you could be waiting months for your first commission cheque. You'll sell stuff to people even if they don't initially want it.

Performance rating:
       1.   2.   3.   4.   5.

6. SELF-MOTIVATED.
Management won't answer questions or attempt to motivate you.

Performance rating:
       1.   2.   3.   4.   5.

7. WE OFFER GREAT BENEFITS.
A library card.

Performance rating:
       1.   2.   3.   4.   5.

8. PENSION/RETIREMENT BENEFITS.
After three years we'll allow you to fund your own pension and, if you behave, we'll give you a five per cent matching contribution.

Performance rating:
       1.   2.   3.   4.   5.

9. SEEKING ENTHUSIASTIC, FUN, HARD-WORKING PEOPLE.

We're looking for people who still live with their parents and won't mind internship-level salaries. Your co-workers are clowns.

Performance rating:

     1.   2.   3.   4.   5.

---

10. CASUAL WORK ATMOSPHERE.

We don't pay enough to expect that you'll dress up – just be washed and clean.

Performance rating:

     1.   2.   3.   4.   5.

---

11. COMPETITIVE ENVIRONMENT.

We have a lot of staff turnover – your co-workers will slit your throat.

Performance rating:

     1.   2.   3.   4.   5.

---

12. EXCITING AND PROFESSIONAL WORK ENVIRONMENT.

Guys in grey suits will bore you with tales of squash and their paintballing weekends on yachts.

Performance rating:

     1.   2.   3.   4.   5.

---

13. MUST BE DEADLINE ORIENTED.

You'll be six months behind schedule on your first day. We're all over the place.

Performance rating:

    1.   2.   3.   4.   5.

---

14. SOME PUBLIC RELATIONS REQUIRED.

If we're in trouble, you'll be prepared to go on national radio/TV and get us out of it.

Performance rating:

    1.   2.   3.   4.   5.

---

15. SOME OVERTIME REQUIRED.

Some time each night and some time each weekend. We don't pay overtime.

Performance rating:

    1.   2.   3.   4.   5.

---

16. SALARY RANGE: € 24,000 TO € 32,000.

We'll offer you € 22,000 to start.

Performance rating:

    1.   2.   3.   4.   5.

---

17. HIGHLY VISIBLE POSITION.

You'll give boring speeches on your own time. If there's a major cock-up you'll be more visible than normal and management will be visible only by their absence.

Performance rating:

    1.   2.   3.   4.   5.

---

18. Flexible hours.
Work 40 hours, get paid for 25. Work 80 hours, get paid for 40.

Performance rating:
    1.   2.   3.   4.   5.

19. Duties will vary.
Anyone in the office can boss you around. You could be preparing the annual report one week and making corned beef sandwiches the next.

Performance rating:
    1.   2.   3.   4.   5.

20. Where employees feel valued.
Those who missed the last round of rightsizing, that is. Nothing like fear to instil values.

Performance rating:
    1.   2.   3.   4.   5.

21. Must have an eye for detail.
We have no quality control. If you screw up and don't spot it, your ass is grass.

Performance rating:
    1.   2.   3.   4.   5.

22. College degree preferred, though not essential.
We're still paying peanuts regardless of how friggin' clever you think you are.

Performance rating:

      1.   2.   3.   4.   5.

---

23. CAREER MINDED.

Female applicants must be childless (and remain that way). Male applicants must talk management like there's no tomorrow.

Performance rating:

      1.   2.   3.   4.   5.

---

24. APPLY IN PERSON.

If you're old, fat or ugly you'll be told the position has been filled. We ain't looking for no bell ringers!

Performance rating:

      1.   2.   3.   4.   5.

---

25. NO PHONE CALLS, PLEASE.

We've filled the job, our call for CVs is just a formality to fill up our human resource database.

Performance rating:

      1.   2.   3.   4.   5.

---

26. SEEKING CANDIDATES WITH A WIDE VARIETY OF EXPERIENCE.

You'll need it to replace three people who, only yesterday, were frogmarched off the premises.

Performance rating:

      1.   2.   3.   4.   5.

---

27. PROBLEM-SOLVING SKILLS A MUST.
Your biggest problem will be to figure out what problems to solve first.

Performance rating:
      1.   2.   3.   4.   5.

---

28. REQUIRES TEAM-LEADER SKILLS.
You'll have the responsibilities of a manager without manager pay, respect or licence to bullshit.

Performance rating:
      1.   2.   3.   4.   5.

---

29. GOOD COMMUNICATIONS SKILLS.
Management communicates, you listen, figure out what they want and do it.

Performance rating:
      1.   2.   3.   4.   5.

---

30. ASPIRATIONS FOR GROWTH WITHIN OUR COMPANY.
Kiss the right asses and you could be looking at paintballing weekends with senior management within your first eighteen months.

Performance rating:
      1.   2.   3.   4.   5.

PERFORMANCE RATING EXPLANATIONS/PSYCHO-MANAGER ANALYSER:

This is one test where the lower your overall score, the better you are as a manager. If you scored between one and 30, you're hot! If you're not already working as a recruitment consultant then you should be. You could also work in real estate or be a team leader in an organised crime circle. You could work in any area of management, from running numbers in Vegas to working in car insurance.

If you scored between 30 and 60, you're still hot but need to brush up on those skills. You could work in human resource management but would need to upgrade the waffle level to break into recruitment or organised crime.

If you scored between 60 and 90, you may be three or four sandwiches short of a picnic but could still make a professional career in management. A few high-impact training weekends could improve your rating substantially (see Chapter 24: X for Extreme Management – it isn't cheap!).

A score of between 90 and 120 is not good and it's time to ask the question as to whether you are suited to the field of management. While some people can get away with a high 'haven't a friggin' clue' rating, most will be screwed over by those with higher ratings.

Finally, if your score is between 120 and 150, you're ready for a career in accountancy and should stay well clear of management.

AUTHOR'S TIP:
Assess your performance at least twice a year with the psycho-manager analyser. If your score is above 60, read this book several times.

CHAPTER 22: V IS FOR VISION

Most managers will be familiar with the term mission statement. The well-seasoned manager will have a mission statement not just for work but for each member of their family, the milkman and their mother-in-law. A vision statement is somewhat different, but despite what it sounds like, does not involve hallucinogenic drugs or insights from a subconscious reality. It simply describes where the business will be in, say, five years' time.

In businesses with long lead times, such as telecommunications, oil exploration or sending a spaceship to the moon, a longer view will nearly always be required.

A vision could be compared to a dream describing future success of the business but with the belief and commitment of the senior executive team to make it into a reality. The vision should harness and focus people's energies towards the chosen goals and set priorities where appropriate.

The vision statement should be short and concise and no more than one page. Management should refer back to it on a regular basis to assess and reassess their progress towards goals. The statement should set out concisely:

1. THE MARKET SEGMENTS AND COUNTRIES:
    1.1 To achieve, maintain or enhance market leadership.
    1.2 To continue investing in and achieving market leadership.

1.3 To enter by organic growth or acquisition as appropriate.

1.4 To cut back, rationalise, downsize, rightsize or exit from.

2. THE COMMERCIAL RATIONALE OF THE COMPANY:

2.1 To describe how the company will be seen by customers and prospective customers as attractively and distinctively different from competitors as possible (differentiation).

For example, all dancers in our lap-dancing joint will be clean and permanent employees, providing a comparable quality and specification with the leading brothels and at a lower price or better quality at the same price, or whenever possible, an innovative service not available elsewhere and priced competitively. Each joint will contain a corporate hospitality suite and provide adequate technical advice and support for all corporate clients on request.

3. ESSENTIAL POLICIES AND QUALITATIVE GOALS:

3.1 Each joint will be autonomous but report into one central head office.

3.2 Sufficient investment will be made in information technology, video, rubber gloves, bathing facilities, etc., to provide a competitive advantage in the marketplace compared with competitors.

3.3 Wherever possible each dancer will be rewarded by an incentive scheme based upon personal achievement.

4. BROAD FINANCIAL PERFORMANCE GOALS. FOR EXAMPLE:

4.1 A minimum of average percentage increase in earnings per share, per dance, each year.

4.2 The proportion of total profits to be achieved from a certain dance within the next five years.

4.3 The percentage return to be achieved on total operating costs within five years.

AUTHOR'S TIP:

Vision statements are important for every single business under the sun. If as a manager you don't have the general wherewithal to visualise where your business will be in five to ten years, consid- *er spending 48 to 96 hours in a sensory deprivation water tank or a combination of drugs and sensory deprivation. If after all your best efforts you still can't visualise where your business will be in the future, you may have to seriously consider becoming an accountant, or an HRM specialist.*

Chapter 23: W is for World-Class Manufacturing

Like roller skating, world-class manufacturing (WCM) management was another management fad of the 1990s. It had to take a back seat and was pushed out of the centre stage by e-manufacturing, e-business and m-business. Granted, the internet and e-mail have revolutionised the world of communications in the same way as the radio, telephone and satellite communications have, but there's more to business than just fast and simplified communications.

One world-class business consultant compared the e-rush of the late 1990s to the gold rush in California in the 1800s. 'Few became millionaires, many perished along the way and many of the success stories related to those that supported the rush or who simply made the journey.' In the California gold rush this would have been the companies that produced carts, guns, wagons, shovels, jeans and beans. In the e-rush the winners were the companies that already had a sound business foundation enhanced by a new presence on the internet and an ability to adapt without screwing up the bread-and-butter business. This makes sense if you're into management big time. But I digress – back to WCM.

WCM is applying the world's best operational practices to the management of manufacturing, reviewing the vital signs (see Chapter 6: Finance: cost, service, inventory) and measuring your business against what's perceived to be the best in the world. It's benchmarking in its truest form on a global basis.

Unfortunately, benchmarking is a dirty word in Ireland and there are huge lobby groups involved. Benchmarking in relation to Ireland is a stitch-up engineered by unions and government, which will see € 1.1 billion handed over to public servants in return for doing their job properly. In real benchmarking, a numeric value is assigned to a given task so that the task can be evaluated and eventually improved. Many public services see this as weeding out the weak, which in a free enterprise economy is not such a bad thing. In a communist country, benchmarking would indeed be a threat to the great balance of things and it would make perfect sense to protect the weak, but in Ireland it only serves to restrain the collective from evolving to something better.

If you're weak in private enterprise, you have two options – improve or move on, shape up or ship out. If you're weak in public enterprise, you have a third option – engage the support of the many to maintain the status quo of the weak.

In the Celtic Tiger economy, public service employees wanted to have salaries benchmarked to rising private enterprise salaries. They wanted equal conditions when salaries were growing at ten to fifteen per cent per annum, but would totally oppose benchmarking when private enterprise wage increases fell below inflation. It's a win-win situation with selective benchmarking.

It was bad enough when Public Service employees' were getting 'an honest week's wage for an honest day's work'. Now, they want their wages and salaries linked to growing private enterprise wages and salaries. However, unions are driving the 'benchmarking' wagon and in Ireland, they're more powerful than government.

BENCHMARKING IN ITS PUREST, NON-BASTARDISED FORM IS GOOD. It improves the way we do things so in turn we're not wondering what the hell went wrong when there's a noticeable exodus of business to developing European countries. Post Celtic Tiger, this exodus of manufacturing is beginning to become apparent. Manufacturing for export, corporate tax on profits of ten per cent is being undercut by the new Europeans offering zero per cent corporate tax on profits to entice multinational corporations to relocate. If they grasp and apply the benchmarking concept faster and better, they'll come out smiling. Private (manufacturing) enterprise will fade into obscurity and public enterprise will be the same as it was last year and the year before and the year before that!

Benchmarking your business couldn't be easier – you just use the measures mentioned earlier in Chapter 6 (cost, service and inventory). Once numeric values are assigned (e.g. cost is ten per cent of total revenue, service is 97 per cent of all orders processed in less than three days and inventory turns 26 times per annum [two weeks' stock]) business can be reviewed and evaluated against competitors within your industry at home and abroad. The mission for the next year may be to bring costs down to eight per cent, service to 98 per cent and inventory turns to 52 times per year – *it isn't rocket science!*

Author's Tip:

Before screwing up your business, practice benchmarking at home with your family. Benchmark the kids' *performance at school, plot on a chart the time everyone gets up at, the amount of television watched versus other more creative pursuits and the number of official family meetings held each week, quarter and year.*

Pie charts, histograms and even Kepner Tregor analysis can be applied to weekly supermarket shopping visits. Have your partner and kids carry out a daily inventory analysis of the fridge and correlate (on a nice chart) what's being eaten versus what's not being eaten! If there's stuff not being eaten on a regular basis, discontinue stocking the product and rationalise your refrigerator product base.

BENCHMARKING, WORLD-CLASS MANUFACTURING AND MANAGEMENT IS AS NORMAL, NATURAL AND ESSENTIAL AS GOOD BOWEL MOVEMENT – practice it and improve yourself and your business.

CHAPTER 24: X IS FOR EXTREME MANAGEMENT

What happens when, as a manager, you've hovered for a prolonged period of time just below your total level of incompetence? (Remember Chapter 16: P is for Peter Principle!) You're tantalisingly close to self-actualisation but just can't conquer the final summit. You've expanded your business and you've rightsized it. You've outsourced all non-essential operations and have run the human resource department the hell out of your company. You've rationalised your product base and service offering and provided an alternative and differentiated market proposition. You've applied key performance indicators and balanced scorecard technique not just to your business, but to your family and friends. You've hired, fired and re-hired people, all in the same day and you've become a paint ball black belt. You've become a management junkie, need more and more but are aware and constrained by the Peter Principle.

QUESTION: what's needed to mount the final summit, fondle the great apex and leap onto the plateau of plateaus or to get into the zone?
ANSWER: extreme management!

Not for the faint-hearted, extreme management puts top management through a rigorous ten-week training session.
Graduates of the 23-hours-a-day, seven-days-a-week course step up to a level of excellence and success that sets them apart from

the rest. It's intensive, it's high impact, it's a diet of coffee, cigars, participative role play and master-level paint ball.

Extreme management gives you the skills to reach the top and never look down. If you ever have to look down it'll only be to urinate on all those below. You'll learn how to:

- Create a sustainable competitive advantage (not just in work but at home with family and with friends).
- Manage in a world of changes yet to come.
- Relax the sphincter and allow your organisation to flourish.
- Establish enduring personal brand and corporate positioning.
- Resolve conflicts – globally.
- Master innovative, battle-tested negotiating techniques.
- Motivate subordinates to embrace change (without HRM waffle).
- Understand and harness the true power of leadership and release the bastard from within.

This is boot camp for management and you could be the prize recruit. Survive the ten weeks of intensive, high-impact training and team paintballing and you'll raise your level of competence – ten-fold.

You'll be equipped to:

- Avoid the traps of management by fashion trend.
- Look after numero uno – you, the manager.
- Select a management style that reflects your personality

and stick with it.
- Think big by not seeking perfection.
- Find your conflict zone – then find a way out.
- Solve a customer problem that wasn't even your fault.
- Keep your customers delighted and gagging for more.

Extreme management training is your executive battlefield passing out, and is worth every euro spent. It's not cheap at € 49,999.99 for the ten-week sabbatical, but delivers tremendous return on investment.

With a well-seasoned accountant you'll get every single euro back, AND MORE, if you pay the right price. The right price is cash, unmarked and untraceable, tightly wrapped in a brown envelope and given to your accountant in a camera-free environment, political donation, Modus Operandi.

Play ball with accountants and they'll claw back the cost plus every government grant and training aid possible. If the accountant is well greased (making a nice little tax-free commission), he or she will ensure all tracks and trails are well covered.

Consultants 'R' Us, based in Slough, London, run the programme twice a year. They look for cash, unmarked and untraceable, up front. Alternatively, some banks will foot the investment if you sign over the deeds of your parents' home. Rest assured, you'll be able to buy ten homes when you graduate!

Dr Cod was a bearded female GP from Kerry. She gave up looking after the sick and injured to became a full-time management uber-guru. She graduated in extreme management in 2002 and now boasts a weekly congregation of 1,200 HR generalists/specialists who worship her extreme management presentations and advanced paint ball demonstrations. The bearded guru talks high-ly of the ten-week grind:

> *I was thrilled with the programme and the training grant was superb. Through some fancy financial footwork I walked away with an extreme training experience, a new career and fifteen grand in my pocket – I'd recommend it to anyone.* It was cer-tainly food for thought, the kind of food you can't get in books.

Unfortunately, there are no other testimonials from course partic-ipants. Most of the other extreme managers reside at bogus UK addresses and couldn't be tracked down for comment or feedback. However, they've all trebled and quadrupled their investment in the first month of graduating the programme.

You'll never regret becoming an extreme manager and it's the only sure route to THE ULTIMATE MANAGEMENT NIRVANA – THE ZONE.

AUTHOR'S TIP:
Falsify property documents, avail of a bogus UK home address, employ an accountant from the fringes of legality and reserve your place on the next extreme management programme.

Chapter 25: Y is the Manager's Greatest Tool

- Why do your competitors do better than you?
- Why do your customers complain?
- Why are your costs higher than they were last year?
- Why use an external recruitment firm when hiring is one of the most critical business activities?

WHY IS THE SINGLE MOST IMPORTANT QUESTION IN MANAGEMENT.

AS A MANAGEMENT STYLE

Jimmy was a manager who capitalised on the full use of 'why' as a management style. For confidentiality, we can't mention Jimmy's second name but he's from Ringsend in Dublin and drives a red VW Jetta.

No matter what you would say to Jimmy, he would always respond in the same manner: 'Why?' Several 'whys' later, he would have peeled back the layers of bullshit and arrived at the core of the issue. As a style it can alienate some people but the benefits of getting to the truth and real agenda far outweigh an occasional puck to the face.

Author's Tip:
Set a target to ask 'why' at least 50 times each day and record it in your filofax or diary. After a

couple of weeks raise the threshold to 100 times per day. Keep raising your threshold for the rest of your life.

Try it out, it really works and is fun. People under the stress and strain of 'why' bombardment may retreat through use of statistics/quantitative techniques. Say nothing, maintain fixed-eye contact and just when they think you've thrown in the towel, give them a short grin-like smile. This response speaks volumes in neurolinguistic programming (fancy name for body language) and what it's saying is, *'You're speaking through your ass.'* Try it, it's fun!

CHAPTER 26: Z IS FOR ZONE - GET INTO IT

THE ZONE IS MANAGEMENT NIRVANA, or in other words, where the individual is at the very peak of their management ability. They are reaching the apex of their understanding of management. On the pyramid of management evolution, the zone is at the top and zonal managers have reached that motivational threshold of self-actualisation.

In the zone, no river is too deep, no mountain too high and *no company too screwed up for a turnaround.*

When in the zone the manager lives that never-say-die attitude and has evolved to become an unstoppable force. They read business plans for breakfast and create them in five minutes, just for the heck of it. It's like second nature.

Although tempted to enter management consultancy and make a killing, they prefer to delegate all the crap work to consultants but will even manage to turn a profit out of that. Unstoppable.

The manager in the zone will be no stranger to downsizing and will rightsize his own business at least three or four times a year or at the first signs of a human resource management department developing. They'll have drained every possible euro out of the business expansion scheme and will have expanded at approximately the same frequency as they downsized. They'll understand the financials, be able to look at a balance sheet without a blank daze and recognise the importance of monotonous, monotone conversation with accountants. They'll not only be familiar with all the academic gurus and management chancers but would qualify themselves to become a guru with a weekend's training.

Only in the zone will the manager truly grasp the greatest and most fundamental flaw in twenty-first century management – human resource management. Having run the HRM department the hell out of their own place, they'll rename all the human resources working for them as people.

They'll recognise extreme management stalemates and know when to apply ignorance management effectively and efficiently, cognisant of the sins of misapplication. Zonal managers will put together job descriptions in seconds and will instantly recognise a private investigator connected to a recruitment firm through a job advertised on the internet.

Most importantly, the manager in the zone will understand the true essence of management, talk it like there's no tomorrow and like they know what the hell they're talking about. They'll never let negativity pull them down and will have no problem lying through their teeth to preserve their ego and kingdom.

While their office, throne and presence will be huge, they'll constantly be reviewing their performance relative to their competence threshold. They'll eat, drink and sleep quality but when they sleep, they'll always do so with one eye open, always aware of recruitment companies, looking for a fast buck.

THE ZONAL MANAGER WILL HAVE A TRUE APPRECIATION FOR SERVICE QUALITY and will instinctively know to bring a flask of coffee, a chair and a wetsuit if travelling on business on an Irish train.

Trained to the very limits of their own ability they'll know every training method possible and will have sucked every euro possible out of government and training authority grants. They'll understand management language and speak with fluency, baffling all those around them. They'll be constantly visualising a better future and translating these visions into comprehensive mission statements, *without the use of drugs and/or sensory deprivation tanks.*

In the zone, the manager is up there on a world-class platform, bull-shitting big time with the best of them. There is no situation on earth they can't waffle out of – no river too deep, no mountain too high. IN THE ZONE THE MANAGER FINALLY DISCOVERS HIS OR HER TRUE SELF, VOCATION AND CALLING. *Only in the zone will he or she make contact and finally release the bastard within.*

At this final stage the manager, as a manager, can learn no more, climb no higher nor swim no deeper.

Next step – become a politican.

In Search of Competence

Glossary

Accountant
A keeper of company and individual financial records characterised with two right brains and an incredibly boring personality. Often described as: arid, characterless, colourless, drab, dull, flat, humdrum, insipid, irksome, lifeless, monotonous, mundane, repetitious, spiritless, stodgy, tedious, tiresome, uninteresting, vapid and wearisome.

Auditor
An accountant who strolls the financial battlefield, post-battle, bayoneting any survivors.

Benchmarking
A business technique whereby business outputs (sales, revenue, profits, etc.), relative to business inputs (cost, headcount, overheads, etc.), are compared to similar business entities, nationally and internationally, as a basis for establishing a focus for business improvement. In relation to public pay awards, it's simply a scam engineered by unions and government, whereby hundreds of millions of euro are given to public service employees in return for them agreeing to do their job properly.

Bonus
Something given to an employee (human resource), above and beyond their normal wage, salary and benefits such as a (totally tax deductible) turkey and ham at Christmas, a cream egg (also tax deductible) at Easter or a brown envelope containing nothing on the first day of April.

Brainstorming
An opportunity to involve employees (human resources) in the overall business management by listening to their suggestions and ideas, regard-

less of how ridiculous, silly or absurd they may seem. It's particularly effective when the manager hasn't a clue what's going on in the overall business.

CASH-COW
A business or part of one that provides steady cash flow. Also slang word for a female accountant.

CATATONIC STUPOR
A dazed, lethargic, indolent or helplessly amazed state brought about by any more than ten minutes conversation with an accountant.

CLIMATE SURVEY
A survey of employees' views, ideas and suggestions, carried out periodically, to update management as to what's going on in the business they're supposed to be managing.

DOBERMAN
A breed of dog developed c.1900 by a German dogcatcher called Herr Doberman, who crossbred stray dogs, intending to produce the meanest, most vicious dog possible. It has a short brown, or black and tan coat, long neck and muzzle and pendulous ears. Generally used in business and management as a last ditch attempt to rid a company of recruitment agencies and/or management consultants.

FOOD-FOR-THOUGHT
A common expression used in business and management when one hasn't a clue what the other person was just talking about. It's the equivalent of a blank, vacant daze in word form – 'Ah, that's certainly food-for-thought – let me get back to you on that'.

FROG-MARCH
This is where a human resource (person) is hustled forward, their arms being held and pinned from behind. It's a particularly popular method employed by managers when removing one of their own, in front of non-

management. It's the modern-day, corporate equivalent of horse-dragging a corpse through the streets.

HUMAN RESOURCE, A
Any man, woman or child of the species 'Homo sapiens', a person, a human being, an individual, a creature, a naked ape, someone, anyone. The term was first applied by HRM specialists in the 1990s, upon a moment of eureka and inconceivable realisation – people were discovered to be an important constituent in organisational success.

MOTIVATION AND THEORY
Motivation is defined as 'the set of forces that cause people to behave in certain ways' – a motivated person (human resource) is a productive employee. Although most of the research theory was carried out in the 1950s, on live human specimens, it only enjoyed a re-emergence in the 1990s with the birth of Human Resource Management and the whole touchy, feely management philosophy.

OBESITY
An excessive amount of corporate fat with the affected company being overweight, the most common organisational disease in affluent, monopolistic and semi-state companies. It's associated with a high mortality rate (not in semi-states) and predisposes to the development of several potentially serious corporate diseases such as the development of an HRM department, sponsorship of bob-sleigh events, building in-house paintball centres, establishing relationships with recruitment companies, etc., etc.

PAINT-BALLING
A game whereby human resources dress up in military clothing, form teams and with paint filled toy guns, mimic the atrocity of war as a means of instilling corporate values such as leadership, team-building and motivation. Other powerful HRM games include team-bungee jumping, team-karaoke and team-synchronised swim demonstrations.

PERSONNEL MANAGEMENT
The forerunner to Human Resource Management and something long thought to be the bastard step-child of accountancy, personnel management was defined by Peter Drucker in 1961 as: 'largely a collection of incidental techniques without much internal cohesion'.

POLITICAL DONATION
A method to legalise the fraudulent transfer of cash for favours sought, usually though not exclusively via a brown envelope, concealed in a tightly wrapped newspaper and delivered in a camera-free environment.

PEOPLE-ON-THE-MOVE COLUMN
A highly effective and inexpensive method of raising the awareness of your business through publishing in newspaper business sections a photo, details and a biography of the latest clown to join your organisation.

RECRUITMENT CONSULTANT
An unscrupulous, corporate, parasitic life form that feeds on the fat of obese, ill-managed companies and semi-state organisations.

SCUMBAG
A contemptible or disgusting person.

TEAM-LEADER
A nebulous, non-descript job title within any organisation, which empowers management responsibility to an individual without management pay, accountability, perks or license to bullshit.

UNIFORM HOMOGENOUS CULTURE
The ultimate nirvana of human resource management where all human resources (people) in the organisation are motivated by HRM practices loosely based on 1950s motivational research and carry out their work diligently, like blissful zombies. For example, the 'excellence thru people' HRM award.